PEEPING TOM

PEEPING TOM
Leo Marks

faber and faber

First published in 1998
by Faber and Faber Limited
3 Queen Square London WC1N 3AU

Photoset by Parker Typesetting Service, Leicester
Printed in England by Clays Ltd, St Ives plc

© Leo Marks, 1998

Photographs © BFI Stills, Posters and Designs, 1997
Portrait on p. vi © Elena Gaussen Marks, 1998
Introduction © Chris Rodley, 1998
Dilys Powell review © New International Syndicate

Leo Marks is hereby identified as author of this work in accordance
with Section 77 of the Copyright, Designs and Patents Act 1988

A CIP record for this book
is available from the British Library

ISBN 0–571–19403–6

2 4 6 8 10 9 7 5 3 1

CONTENTS

Portrait by Elena Gaussen Marks of Michael Powell (left)
and Leo Marks (right)

INTRODUCTION
Leo Marks interviewed by Chris Rodley, 1998

I first met Leo Marks in 1978, at his place. I remember a dark room, the smell of cigar smoke, and a face half in shadow, half in the dim light of a cluttered London mansion-block apartment. and then there was the rich, hypnotic voice, which seemed to emanate from the impossibly deep recesses of the studded leather armchair in which he sat: the voice of someone both understanding and enquiring. The encounter felt like some form of psychic surgery, during which it was difficult to tell exactly who was asking the questions, and who was providing the answers.

I had tracked down the shadowy creator of *Peeping Tom* because there was so much to ask. Nothing, however, could have prepared me for the meeting. To a would-be cinephile in a movie brat world, it was oddly shocking to discover that Leo Marks had lived an extraordinary life prior to, and completely outside of, his involvement with the cinema and *Peeping Tom*. His own story began to sound as remarkable and unlikely as that of his creation and near-namesake, Mark Lewis.

To get the full account, the public will have to wait for Marks' typically unorthodox and imposing autobiography, *Between Silk and Cyanide* (HarperCollins, 1998). Ten years in the writing, it will surprise and amaze, as well as upset a few official histories on the operations of the intelligence community during World War II. For this is where – as head of codes and cyphers for SOE (Special Operations Executive) – Marks' own story takes flight. It's also where his remarkable achievements began. Moreover, his covert war-time activities, unique in themselves, were to provide the unlikely inspiration for *Peeping Tom*, originally conceived in 1943 in fearful circumstances.

The making and breaking of codes is central to Marks' life. He worked for SOE from June 1942 until the end of the war. SOE was credited by General Eisenhower with shortening the war by three months, and he paid particular tribute to its communications. But to Leo Marks it came at 'great and unquantifiable cost'. A brilliant mathematician and cryptographer, Marks was also an artist and intellectual – a powerful and potentially explosive combination when fighting a battle of wits for the liberation of Europe. His responses and solutions to the 'spirit of Resistance' were as uniquely imaginative as those of Michael Powell and Emeric Pressburger when, at the suggestion of the Ministry of Information, they made a film to promote Anglo-American relations at the end of the war. The result of that particular patriotic brief was the gloriously fantastical *A Matter of Life and Death*. It's perhaps no real surprise, therefore, that Marks and Powell should eventually find each other.

If the movie *Peeping Tom* is a complex, cinematic labyrinth of signs, clues and references – a Chinese-box puzzle just waiting to be solved – it's because it was written that way. Marks conceived the film, shot by shot, with alarming visual, as well as verbal, specificity. Nothing was left to chance, and little to interpretation. For those comforted by artistic intentionality, *Peeping Tom* is heaven-sent.

It would be inaccurate to suggest that Powell merely filmed what was on the page, but *Peeping Tom*'s shooting script does read more like a *post*-production script. It seems that Powell not only recognized a good thing when he saw it, but guaranteed its safe passage to the screen in all its most important aspects – adding both to its power and to its moral complexity by virtue of his own empathy with Mark Lewis.

The unanimous press antipathy that greeted *Peeping Tom* on its initial release in 1960 is both well documented and easy to ridicule now that the film is recognized as one of British cinema's most remarkable and aberrant achievements. Film critics of the time were unable or unwilling to deal with the film's *ideas*, seeking refuge in what they considered to be *Peeping Tom*'s 'trash' aesthetic, its over-theatrical secondary performances, and its taboo subject matter, which – for them – evidently proved once and for all just how sadistic and unpleasant Michael Powell really was.

They were certainly unwilling to 'read' the film; to decipher the many messages that Marks had encoded in both text and imagery. *Peeping Tom* was not only born of Marks' wartime experiences in the briefing rooms of the Code Department during the war, it is, in itself, a highly codified film. By splicing his twin interests in cryptography and Freudian psychology, Marks created a complex anti-hero: an 'indecipherable'. Mark Lewis is at once deeply sympathetic and monstrous. If we are to understand him, we must pay attention to everything he says and does. Nothing is irrelevant or insignificant. He is not himself. He is a mess of clues. His true character, desires and motivations must be uncovered by the audience. You have to look long and hard at a coded message written on a blackboard in order to perceive the *actual* message staring you in the face.

As SOE's Codemaster in WWII, Leo Marks wrote many original poems for agents. These verses functioned as codes, to be used in the field. The most famous was given to the agent Violette Szabo, a courageous crack-shot agent despatched to work with the French Resistance. Her heroism, capture and tragic death were eventually immortalised by the film *Carve Her Name With Pride* (1958). In that movie, Virginia McKenna – playing Szabo – recited the agent's hitherto unheard code-poem 'The Life That I Have' just before her execution. Public response to the verse was overwhelming, and although Marks had forbidden the film-makers to reveal its author, it was only a matter of time before his cover was blown.

For some, it is hard to reconcile the fact that the author of the Szabo code-poem and the writer of *Peeping Tom* are one and the same person. Perhaps Marks is the greatest indecipherable of all: a man who dedicated himself to saving lives during WWII with chalk, a blackboard and 400 coders; the man chosen by Martin Scorsese to provide the voice of the Devil for his film *The Last Temptation of Christ*; the man who – with *Peeping Tom* – created one of the most chilling meditations on the nature of cinema we're ever likely to see. And the man who, even when composing codes for agents, could so poetically convey what was truly a matter of life and death:

> The life that I have
> Is all that I have
> And the life that I have
> Is yours.
>
> The love that I have
> Of the life that I have
> Is yours, and yours, and yours.

A sleep I shall have
A dream I shall have
Yet death will be but a pause.
For the peace of my years
In the long green grass
Will be yours, and yours, and yours.

CHRIS RODLEY: *Few people know that the writer of* Peeping Tom *was heir to perhaps the most famous bookshop in the world. What's the connection between an antiquarian booksellers and one of the most 'scandalous' British movies?*

LEO MARKS: About three months before I was born, Father decided that I was to run his rare bookshop. 84 Charing Cross Road was the address and Marks and Co. was the name. Not because it was a company. His partner was called Cohen, and they decided it sounded rather better if they called it Marks and Co. And as Mr Cohen had no sons, and I was my father's only one, I was destined to run it shortly before birth.

So every Saturday morning from the age of eight onwards, I was brought by my father to 84 Charing Cross Road to learn the value, the price, the cost and the profit of rare books. And as a reward, every Saturday afternoon, Mother would take me to the cinema, up the road to the Astoria. So the association between books and the cinema was born at the age of eight. But something was suddenly added to it.

One morning he showed me a first edition of Edgar Allan Poe's *The Gold Bug*. He told me it had cost £6.50, and that it was going to be priced at £850, because he was in a generous mood that day. And I began reading *The Gold Bug*, and it was about codes – the first time I'd ever heard about codes. And when I looked at the back of the book, I found that Marks and Co. had put the cost of the book *in* code, which they did at the back of all their books. And as Dad had told me it cost £6.50, I was able to work out their code. I then decided that one day I wanted to understand codes and write a horror story, like Edgar Allan Poe.

CR: *Codes were to become central to your life and work, but how did you 'break in' to cryptography?*
LM: Because I didn't want to run Father's shop, when war finally started I said to the Ministry of Labour that I wanted to be a cryptographer. They didn't know the word, but I ended up in a school for code breakers, which I found was very much a course for accountants. I didn't feel this was the way to learn to *devise* codes, which interested me a little more than breaking them. They weren't quite sure what to do with me. I wasn't a very good pupil but one day I managed, entirely by mistake, to break a code in a few hours that was supposed to take several days.

CR: *You very quickly became involved in cryptography at the highest level, as part of the war effort. How did that come about?*
LM: Well, there was this potty organization in Baker Street called Inter-services Research Bureau, and they had a vacancy for someone who might know a bit about codes. So I was sent for an interview. This was in fact Special Operations Executive (SOE), which controlled all the Resistance movements in Europe. During the interview I realized that the very senior gentleman cross-examining me believed I was the son of Sir Simon Marks (Marks and Spencer). And because SOE occupied premises owned by Sir Simon Marks I realized that what we *really* wanted were canteen facilities! I was given the job and a few days later SOE got their canteen facilities. I've lived off the credit ever since.

CR: *What was it about codes that fascinated you so much?*
LM: The fact that so much depended on their being safe. And it was a strange challenge. I felt at home with them. As every book in Marks and Co. valued above £5 had a code in the back of it, and this was the kingdom I was supposed to inherit; I ignored the books and inherited the codes.

CR: *I gather your parents weren't aware of the very important work you were doing.*
LM: No. My father was an appalling security risk. Had he known what I was doing it would have been all over London, and his favourite restaurant. So he believed I worked in the Ministry of Labour.

CR: *You've told me that Sigmund Freud once visited 84 Charing Cross Road, and that you became a devotee. What was your interest in Freud's teachings?*

LM: When I joined SOE I was twenty-two, Jewish, and didn't want to accept a junior commission because I might have to say 'Sir' and not mean it. An interest in Freud was almost instinctive, in an only child destined to run a book shop, hooked on codes, The greatest code of all was the unconscious, and Freud appeared to have deciphered it. Perhaps not accurately, altogether, but what an attempt he'd made!

CR: *Could you elaborate on this connection between codes and psychoanalysis?*

LM: I was interested in psychotherapy, just before the war broke out, but also in codes, and discovered that whilst psychotherapy is the study of the secrets a person keeps from him or herself, codes are the study of secrets nations keep from each other.

CR: *When you joined SOE, you set about revolutionizing their approach to the 'code war'. What exactly did you do?*

LM: The problem with SOE was that every single agent who went into the field had to choose and memorize a poem, and that poem was to use as a code. Trouble was, a boy scout could break them! The system was highly insecure. If the Germans cracked a message, they could mathematically reconstruct the five words on which it had been encoded. One poor chap had chosen the National Anthem. Now if the Germans recovered 'Save', 'Our', 'God', 'Gracious' and 'King', they would know what verse he was using and could read all his messages without further effort.

So I *insisted* that as many code poems as possible should be original compositions, so that at least the Germans could not foretell what the rest of the code was going to be. And because SOE was very reluctant to provide any, I wrote some myself, and used to put them in what I called the 'Ditty Box' for agents to use – though most of them preferred well-known quotations, which they'd learnt at school.

CR: *Perhaps your major contribution to the 'code war' was your invention of the 'silk code'. Could you say something about how this worked?*

LM: If an agent was caught in the field, their code poem could be tortured out of them, and all their traffic read. It took me twelve months to convince SOE that every single agent must have a code printed on silk, every single one of them different, so that as they sent the message they could cut it away from the silk, burn it, and because they couldn't remember them, the codes could *not* be tortured out of them. But if they lost their silk codes, they had to have a poem in reserve.

CR: *You put together a unique department comprising only women. How did that happen?*

LM: Well, the major nightmare in Baker Street was that if an agent went into the field, they'd have no electric light, no squared paper, maybe had forgotten their poem, and the German direction-finding cars might be going around the area. So they'd make mistakes in their coding. Now, when I joined SOE, if an agent sent a message that London could not decipher, London would simply say: 'You've made a mistake, repeat that message.' So the agent would re-encode it, and get caught in the process of retransmitting it.

So I made a rule that there should be *no* such thing as an indecipherable message, and got a team of 400 girls, and we would work round the clock to break a message if it seemed indecipherable. One took us 750,000 attempts before we broke it. And we always had to work against the clock.

CR: *Could you say something about how your wartime work with agents was to eventually inspire* Peeping Tom?

LM: The first thing for which an agent would be tortured would be his – or her – code and security check. And it was torture knowing this. So before going to brief an agent for the last time, I tried to develop an 'inner ear'. Because the best communication is unconscious; what the unconscious *says* to the unconscious. So I would stand outside the briefing room building for ten minutes to try to forget every other anxiety, in order to belong *completely* to the agent, and pick up what I could.

When I was sure they knew how to use their silk codes and their poems, I set them some exercises. Now, all I had to do during those exercises was to watch them, unobtrusively; to 'photograph' them when they were coding. So I would either spend that time mentally writing poems for the 'Ditty Box', or developing something else, and so the idea of writing *Peeping Tom* was born in the briefing rooms of SOE.

I became convinced that all cryptographers are basically voyeurs. And in my case, I was staring at these agents. I wanted to remember them – in case they sent an indecipherable message back – watching them, probing them, *trying* to belong to them. And so the idea of a voyeur was born.

CR: *Why, when you eventually came to write the script for* Peeping Tom, *did you decide to make Mark Lewis a focus puller and photographer?*

LM: I knew nothing whatsoever about photography, but every single code had to be printed onto silk, and they were all different. Although they knew how to mass-produce maps on silk, this was a new technique. So I became obsessed by photography, and even more obsessed by how to persuade photographers to work around the clock so that every agent could have a code printed on silk that was unique to him, or her. That is why Peeping Tom became a photographer.

CR: *At a crucial point in the film, Mark says to Helen: 'Do you know what the most frightening thing in the world is? It's fear.' Indeed, the whole film spins on notions of fear. Where did that theme come from?*

LM: Every briefing room was full of it. The bravest agents were afraid only of failing their comrades. They weren't afraid of torture; they were reconciled to it. Those who weren't afraid of anything were the ones *we* were frightened of.

So Peeping Tom wanted to photograph the impossible, the way I wanted to create the impossible – unbreakable codes. And what he finally wanted to do was frighten people to death – *in his own way* – and photograph them.

CR: *You once told me that you wrote a very strange-sounding report after the war was over; a kind of Freudian reading of wartime activities in your department.*

LM: At the end of the war, each Department Head was required to write a very full official account of their work. I wrote three. One was about our coding activities around the world – sometimes in places where we were not supposed to be. The second, top-secret report was on the truth about Holland which has, to this day, never been disclosed – the truth as the Code Department knew it. A truth we have never told. That was a fifteen-page report, one copy only.

The third report I wrote was entitled 'Cyphers, Signals and Sex'. Thinking I understood Freud's teachings, and everything to do with the unconscious, it was about why the most reliable coders sometimes made the most appalling mistakes at peculiar times, and the reasons why agents failed to bury their parachutes. I believed that some agents had an unconscious will to self-destruct, and an unconscious will to fail. It was something one sensed. Some of them made mistakes so elementary they couldn't be accounted for in terms of tension or anxiety. Their lives depended on burying their parachutes. And I regarded the act of dropping as an act of gestation. There was no time then to explore, deal with, or acknowledge the unconscious resistance in a Resistance Movement agent.

CR: *You mentioned the coders as well. What puzzled you about them?*
LM: Well, I couldn't understand why some of my best coders were spasmodically totally unreliable. Their commanding officer said that perhaps it was to do with their periods. I thought she meant moon periods! She very kindly elaborated, but I wanted to know the dates of those periods. She regarded this as absolutely top secret, offensive, and we daren't ask. So I did a little arithmetical homework, noting when these very dangerous mistakes were made, and got a rough idea of when the girls' periods were due. I made a note in code on my desk to give them light work at this time. We had stumbled upon premenstrual tension.

Later, when I wanted access to my original reports I had an official letter from the Foreign Office which said they could find no trace of my main report, nor could they find my Dutch report, but they were pleased to tell me they did have a copy of a report called 'Cyphers, Signals and Sex'. and someone had put a sticker on that report saying: 'To be preserved as a document of historical importance.' But someone else had crossed out 'historical' and put 'hysterical', and on reading it again I decided they were right.

CR: *It sounds as if you were a very precocious young man.*

LM: SOE was a precocious organization. The greatest asset was the precocity of the girls. They were all young. I was slightly younger than most. Apart from the 400 coders, who worked round the clock, I had a team of twelve very carefully selected female briefing officers. And they were very attractive, because when they went to brief agents, I wanted their faces to be those the agents would remember under torture, rather than mine. These briefing offices would get agents out of bed in the early hours of the morning to take them through their codes. And if they thought of ways of making those occasions even more memorable, I very much hoped they would use them! Baroness Hornsby-Smith, personal assistant to Lord Selborne, our minister, christened the girls 'Marks' Harem', regrettably with no justification.

CR: *What was your relationship with the girls?*

LM: I used to lecture them about once a fortnight just to keep the pressure up, and did everything I could to impress them. Once I managed to do the *Times* crossword in front of them in under four minutes. What I didn't tell them was that I had set it myself!

CR: *Why was it necessary to play tricks on them?*

LM: To conceal my absolute terror of every single one of them! They were frightened, we all were. I'd never been abroad – well, once. I was an only child, spoilt rotten. I used to pretend how much I wanted to go to war, but I didn't have the courage, and never would have had the courage. I was happy to be right at the back of the back room. And most of the girls came from very sheltered homes. There they were, in the country, breaking messages they didn't understand, saving the lives of agents they never met. We had a certain closeness.

CR: *Where did you get these girls from?*

LM: We relied on the FANYs* to provide the mainstream of our

---

* FANY: First Aid Nursing Yeomanry. Originally a small unit of nurses, founded in 1907. During WWI they ran Field Hospitals, drove ambulances and set up soup kitchens. In WWII, some 2,000 FANYs provided the backbone to SOE's operations, working in cyphers and signals, as agent-conducting officers and as agents in the field, primarily in France.

coders. They were set exams and I interviewed most of them before they were accepted. But we also relied on the Labour Exchange. It was very difficult to describe to them the qualities we needed, so I wrote an official memo: 'Do not reject any girls on the grounds of insanity without first offering her to SOE.' The supply almost kept up with the demand. They were a very special team, unlike any other.

If a girl said she liked music, enjoyed crossword puzzles but was hopeless at arithmetic, I would accept her at once. That meant she'd been taught arithmetic badly at school, but had that feeling for rhythm so essential to a coder.

CR: *I gather that some of them were very eccentric . . .*
LM: We had one girl whom I thought was a coding genius. I insisted on promoting her to an officer. But there was one major problem with her. All her life she'd been brought up with horses; to her, the whole world consisted of horses, and now she was deprived of her beloved creatures and put in a lonely station in the country. So she used to make up for this by galloping round the grounds every morning, neighing like a horse! I didn't mind this, provided she continued to be the exemplary coder that she was.

One day, General Gubbins, head of SOE, announced that he was going to visit the station. I warned the girl not to be put off, that he was really a very kind, highly brilliant man, and that she should just answer his questions. But when he asked her one, she looked at him and just neighed! The CO of the station phoned me and said: 'Come and take your bloody horse away!' She was beyond price. So yes, it was full of eccentrics.

CR: *I also gather that some of them claim you brainwashed them, and that they have no memory whatsoever of the work they did for you during those years. Is that true?*
LM: Their brains didn't so much need washing as cleansing! I was worried about certain secrets to which they were party, which in those days would have been highly inconvenient if disclosed. So I tried a little experiment with three coders and a briefing officer in order to induce amnesia about the work they had done for the Code Department. But if you're on the verge of asking me what that experiment was, I have brainwashed myself into forgetting it!

CR: *When you decided to write* Peeping Tom, *why did you decide to approach Michael Powell to direct it, and how did you get to meet him?*
LM: I wanted to meet Michael Powell because he'd directed *A Matter of Life and Death* and *The Red Shoes*, among others. Michael Powell was the film industry's Resistance Movement. *A Matter of Life and Death* was, I think, his masterpiece, and I regarded *Peeping Tom* as a matter of death and death.

I managed to get an introduction to him through a very influential lady agent who'd agreed, reluctantly, to look after me, if I insisted on writing a film script or two. She also looked after Graham Greene, so I think she knew what she was doing. Michael Powell knew damn-all about me, and it was like talking to a camera. I didn't know that completely unknown authors were not supposed to go to world-renowned directors and recount every single shot in a film they want to write. But I had the whole shooting script of *Peeping Tom* in my mind. You have to think visually if you're interested in codes. So I told it to him, shot by shot.

At the end he looked at me in complete silence. So I thought: 'Right, I've made a mess of that, I'll try another one.' So I recited a second film I wanted to write. Every single scene. And this 'camera' continued to regard me in complete silence. So I thought: 'What have I got to lose; I'll try a third.' So I did, and still no response from Mr Powell. So I got up and said: 'Please forgive me for wasting your time. May I tell you how much pleasure your films gave Resistance Movement agents when they most needed it.' And he said: 'My dear chap, my voice is in my throat, sit down. They're all mine!'

So I went rushing back to my agent saying, 'He wants all of them!' And she said, 'Darling, don't you think you ought to wait and see how the first one turns out?' But knowing everything in those days I said: 'No. It's a three-picture deal, because he mightn't like it when it turns out.' So three films were committed to Michael Powell. And that was the birth of *Peeping Tom*.

CR: *How did the production begin to shape up?*
LM: Powell's last few films had lost a great deal of money; he'd split from his partner Emeric Pressburger (they were the most productive team in the history of the British film industry), and

then he encountered *Peeping Tom*. Now, the script was so bad that three major film companies tried to buy it from him! That was a new experience for Micky. Two offered to finance him, an even newer experience. And then Laurence Harvey, who'd just made *Room at the Top*, wanted to play the lead. So Micky could not have had an easier time. But being Micky, he quarrelled with each of them in turn, and ended up with a small production company. And instead of Laurence Harvey, he cast a German actor, Carl Boehm.

CR: *I gather you were not at all happy with Powell's casting of Boehm. Why was that?*

LM: Harvey, a very skilful actor indeed, was likely to have made Mark more of a narcissist, and probably a fringe homosexual. He would have given him depth. So did Boehm. My only objection to Boehm was that I couldn't reconcile his German accent with his father's perfect English. Carl phoned me from the studio after filming the final scene and said: 'Leo, Mark is dead.' And I said: 'Carl, he's not yet been born.' Few authors are satisfied with an artist's interpretation of a part they've created.

CR: *Peeping Tom* takes delight in playing many games, some of them based on names. The fictional director, for instance, is called Arthur Baden. If one puts his name with Micky's, you get Baden-Powell – that all-important figure in the lives of many little boys. Is that why Mark Lewis is like an anagram of Leo Marks?

LM: If you try to anagram my name out of Mark Lewis, you're going to have a very, very long job on your hands. There is no reason, of which I'm aware, that Mark Lewis has a subjective connotation, although my identification with him couldn't be much greater in terms of what he suffered, and what he tried to do about it.

CR: *What is Mark's problem?*

LM: His father was his problem. His father was a psychiatrist obsessed with fear. He was interested in the cause of fear, in the responses to fear, and he experimented on his little boy. He photographed him at all hours of the day and night. He would wake him up and frighten him, and photograph his responses. Mark grew up obsessed with fear, and grew up to be a voyeur.

CR: *Much has been made of the fact that Powell used his own son, Columba, as the young Mark, and played the evil father himself. Critics of the time singled this out as one of the reasons they were repelled by the film. Why do you think Powell did that?*

LM: Michael would have used his daughter in the lead if he'd had a daughter! He had major budgetary problems, and it appealed to him to play the demoniacal father. He directed himself superbly, and he handled his little boy with great skill. So it was partly budgetary, partly emotional. It was Powell's way of showing that he really did understand the script.

CR: *There are many mysterious and extremely effective touches in film, such as when Mark imitates the actions of others. What is that particular action about?*

LM: Introjection. A complete identification with the person he is involved with. He will copy their movements, their inflections. He will become that person. He is photographing them, copying everything they do. It's his way of becoming one with them, and they're very lucky if he doesn't decide to destroy them as well. Introjection is a symptom of scoptophilia – the morbid urge to gaze. The identification is complete. Mark's not even aware he's doing this. He can't help it. Nor would he if he could. And Mark – like Michael Powell – was a walking camera.

CR: Peeping Tom *appears to be a highly codified work. One suspects that everything has a reason to be there, even if that reason is not immediately clear. Is that true?*

LM: It was conceived in a code room, surrounded by agents being briefed. I suppose the contemporary word is 'depth'. Depth has a special meaning in cryptography. If Mark does have depth, then I have partially succeeded in creating the agony of a Peeping Tom.

It was an adventure in film-making. It broke a few rules, the way we broke them in coding. And in coding, when you create a code, all that matters is that the enemy doesn't break it.

I believe that the cinema makes voyeurs of us all. And I wanted to write a study of one particular voyeur, from a little boy to the time that he died. I wanted to show, visually, what made him a Peeping Tom, and scatter throughout that as many visual clues as I could find, in the hope that the audience would want to discover the clear text of this man's code for themselves.

At the very end of the war, many agents had been tortured. This was a new experience for British Intelligence. The problem was, how to help them? We went up and down Harley Street, and learnt the hard way what did and did not work in psychotherapy. And we discovered that the language of dreams – the code of dreams – was the most important of all to break. Freud had discovered one method. There were others. But the fundamental lesson was: there is a secret message in every code known as a dream.

CR: Peeping Tom *is very un-British in at least one important respect: its concentration on sex and sexual impulses. Would you agree?*
LM: At the time of writing *Peeping Tom* I did believe most of it was sexual. And though I still think a great deal of it is, today I believe it to be unconscious, not *necessarily* sexual. *Peeping Tom* is full of Mark's own sexual inclinations, some of which he satisfies himself. He found staring at the photographs he'd taken very, very exciting, and he would reach a pinnacle of excitement watching them. Like Michael Powell, he was the last of the independents! But Mark was a man whose tensions were unsupportable.

CR: *Did you have many discussions with Powell about the* meaning *of film?*
LM: Oh no, no, no, no. To Michael Powell, this was the ultimate exercise in his craft – of photographing the impossible. For him, to be asked to photograph the impossible as part of a story was the climax of a career. The story and the characters were of secondary consideration, which is why he allowed the script full reign. Anything that is right with *Peeping Tom* really is Powell's, and anything that is wrong is mine, because of the script. He regarded it as a tender love story, and I was happy to let him have that illusion.

CR: *One aspect of the script that is missing from the final film is any sense of the 'documentary of fear' that Mark is actually making. Could you say something about that?*
LM: One of the problems with *Peeping Tom* is that Micky, having quarrelled with so many people in the film industry, was limited to a very small budget. But he decided that he'd like a big name in the film. Carl Boehm had no name whatsoever so, having made a

film with Moira Shearer, he decided he wanted a scene written that would give her the chance to dance. There was only one place in the whole film for this, and I did not want to change it. That's because what was there in the script was the most important disclosure about Mark in the entire film: why he's driven to frighten people to death, to achieve the impossible. Instead of which, I was required to write a dance sequence for Miss Shearer to perform. That was the first time Micky pulled rank, and indicated that it was very important that this should happen. So I shelved the original scene. In the original script I disclose what Mark's film really would have been, which tells a great deal about him. I'd been down to the studio once to watch a day's shooting. In coding I learnt that there is only one captain, and I realized that this was even more true of a film studio, and never went back. Powell was the Captain. Powell had to do it as he saw it. And he did.

CR: *Why does Mark only kill women?*
LM: He would be particularly interested in frightening women to death, having been photographed at the deathbed of his mother. It was ultimately his sexual expression, until he meets one girl – played in the film by Anna Massey – the first person towards whom he has no such impulses. He dreads getting to know her in case they start. He doesn't want to hurt her. Unhappily they cut a scene from the film between the two of them in a restaurant where you begin to understand that Mark is falling in love, and is capable of love. That was cut out. I think it helped to make room for Moira Shearer's dance!

Right at the end, when he knows he's going to die, he is so relieved that he's not going to kill Anna Massey. He knows it's his turn. All the cameras his father ever used are going off around him, and he knows he's going to disclose to himself that moment when he is terrified of dying.

CR: *When you finally saw the completed film, did it surprise you in any way?*
LM: Yes, that it was ever made! The whole of the film was seen in Michael Powell's house, shot by shot, before he ever reached for his camera. So nothing was a surprise, except what finally was cut from the film, which might have added to an understanding of

Mark – what it was he really wanted to film when he was alone in that film studio with Moira Shearer. I miss that.

CR: *What was Powell like to work with?*

LM: Micky was an extraordinary man to work with. It was possible to ring him at three o'clock in the morning, and if it was important or difficult enough, he didn't mind a bit. There was one scene he very much liked. I did too: it was a dialogue scene. I phoned him at three o'clock one morning and said: 'Micky, could we cut that whole scene, and just have a shot of Peeping Tom kissing his camera?' 'It's in!' he said. And although I submitted every single shot in the film to him in script form, he didn't mind.

And when I asked the impossible of him, he made it happen. Like one particular scene, where Peeping Tom is up a gantry in the film studio and I describe pencils falling from his pocket and landing like torpedoes at the foot of the Police Inspector. To me, those falling pencils were agents dropping into the field, and codes being dropped with them. Powell made that happen.

CR: *Powell had, in some respects, a very bad reputation as a director: temper tantrums, humiliations, etc. Did you see any of that?*

LM: Well, Micky had a hotel in the South of France, and he used to say that the two most expensive luxuries in his life were paying me and running the hotel. But one of the reasons the hotel was running at a loss is that if he didn't like the people who tried to stay there he wouldn't admit them. He was as selective of his guests as he was of his artists. And occasionally of his writers. He was a giant talent with a pygmy generosity; a very incisive, and in some ways a very cold man. But the miracle was that he was also a compassionate man, and it was that mixture that dwarfed so many other directors.

CR: *It's uncanny that, at the same time as* Peeping Tom *was being made, Hitchcock was making* Psycho – *another remarkable and unfashionably sympathetic portrayal of a serial killer. Did you know that Mark Lewis had, in Norman Bates, an American counterpart of sorts?*

LM: I was sent for by Alfred Hitchcock, who said he'd heard I'd written a very interesting script which had run into some trouble as a film. He was having difficulties with *Psycho* and would very much like to meet me, if I was going to Hollywood. I was very tempted to, but other events intervened. Michael Powell was the best director for *Peeping Tom*. He wasn't the best director of Michael Powell, but he knew what that film needed.

CR: *What did you make of the unanimous, hysterical and completely unsympathetic critical reaction to* Peeping Tom *on its eventual release?*

LM: A great many of the responses to *Peeping Tom* were typical of the public responses then to Peeping Toms. They were sent to prison. No attempt whatsoever was made to understand them. And with *Peeping Tom* we sought not merely understanding but sympathy, because this little boy had been butchered. He grew up not minding what happened to him, knowing he would be caught, unable to stop himself, because there was no one to help him. The critics did not seem prepared for this, especially from a minor film company at eleven o'clock in the morning.

The critics saw the film, I believe, mid-morning – some of them were sober – and apparently they were expecting to see something crude and violent and salacious. The company which actually made the film had a reputation for cheap horror stories. They were not expecting to see anything remotely serious, and they reacted very subjectively. One very respected critic called Dilys Powell came up to me after the press show and said: 'Don't you do that again!'

Many, many years later, when she was in her eighties, she recanted in the *Sunday Times* – which is wonderful for a woman of that age, that upbringing and that prestige. She re-reviewed *Peeping Tom* and hoped to apologize to Michael Powell. But then she died.

CR: *What was the reaction of your own mother and father?*

LM: As close to suicide as it was possible to go! I was an only child, and never allowed to go away – physically or mentally. The press reviews absolutely shocked them. During the war, someone put a white feather through our letter box, because I was a civilian, and it was thought I was shirking the war effort. To me that was excellent security. To my parents, this was total war. Suspecting they knew who'd sent it, they declared war on them. But when there were appalling reviews for 'Peeping Tom', they were so

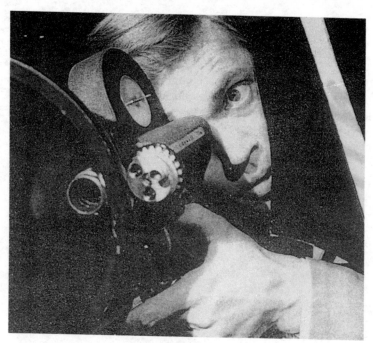

Sunday Times, June 1994

Misunderstood: Carl Boehm's cameraman is obsessed with death

Dilys Powell's film of the week

Peeping Tom (Wednesday, Sky Movies Gold, 10pm)
Michael Powell has long been known as one of this country's most distinguished film-makers. But when, in 1960, he made a horror film, I hated the piece and, together with a great many other British critics, said so. Today, I find I am convinced that it is a masterpiece. If in some afterlife conversation is permitted, I shall think it my duty to seek out Michael Powell and apologise. Something more than a change of taste must exist.

The original story and screenplay come from Leo Marks; at their centre is a cameraman (played by Carl Boehm) whose scientist father used him in childhood in a study of fear. The boy grows up obsessed by images of the human face frozen in extremes of terror. He multiplies them by himself photographing death, and, in fact, becoming a multiple killer.

With so gifted a director this can hardly be anything but a frightening movie, but its object is the examination of emotion and not titillation. Interesting that it should be revived now when there has been much concern about the influence of cinema. All the more reason to distinguish between the serious and the merely sensational horror. Reading now what I wrote in 1960 I find that, despite my efforts to express revulsion, nearly everything I said conceals the extraordinary quality of Peeping Tom. See it, and spare a moment to respect the camerawork of Otto Heller.

ashamed. I tried to prevent them from seeing it, but there was no way. They never quite forgave *Peeping Tom*.

CR: *Do you think Powell was hurt by the response?*
LM: Oh no, no, no. He regarded himself as a life-long educator! He was surprised, but he wasn't hurt, because his opinion of the contemporary critics was not a high one. Powell would never permit himself anything as mundane as disappointment.

Peeping Tom

Note: This is the original script from which *Peeping Tom* finally emerged.

Peeping Tom was released in the UK in 1960. The cast and crew was as follows:

MARK LEWIS	Carl Boehm
HELEN STEPHENS	Anna Massey
VIVIAN	Moira Shearer
MRS STEPHENS	Maxine Audley
DORA	Brenda Bruce
MILLY	Pamela Green
LORRAINE	Susan Travers
MR PETERS	Bartlett Mullins
TONY HUNTER	Brian Wallace
DON JARVIS	Michael Goodliffe
ARTHUR BADEN	Esmond Knight
DIANE ASHLEY	Shirley Anne Field
INSPECTOR GREGG	Jack Watson
SERGEANT MILLER	Nigel Davenport
DR ROSEN	Martin Miller
ELDERLY GENTLEMAN	Miles Malleson
PUBLICITY CHIEF	Maurice Durant
ASSISTANT DIRECTOR	Brian Worth
MISS SIMPSON	Veronica Hurst
STORE DETECTIVE	Alan Rolfe
MARK'S FATHER	Michael Powell

Directed by	Michael Powell
Produced by	Michael Powell
Director of Photography	Otto Heller
Original Story and Screenplay	Leo Marks
Editor	Noreen Ackland
Designed by	Arthur Lawson
Sound and Music by	Brian Easdale

The action of the story is in full colour; Mark's own films and his father's film, projected in the course of the action, are in black and white.

The screen remains dark for a moment.

In the darkness we hear the film's theme music – a gentle whirring purring noise . . . nothing to be alarmed about . . . it might be a small contented motor . . .

FADE IN:

EXT. A DESERTED STREET. NIGHT

LONG SHOT *of the solitary figure of a Woman standing professionally alone at the end of the street.*

It is a bright, still night . . . We can hear the Woman whistling 'Stardust' merrily to herself . . .

Camera tracks towards her . . . A Man's footsteps are overlaid . . .

We hear the Man start to whistle 'Stardust' under his breath – haltingly at first, then in time with the Woman . . .

5

As we approach, she glances at us over her shoulder – then turns round for a better look –

Her whistling stops . . . so, at the same moment, does the man's –

CLOSE SHOT *of Dora – a plump, attractive brunette – still young enough to need two glances at the customers . . .*

She smiles at us – and is pleased with the reception . . . She hesitates for a long moment, weighing us up carefully . . . and then – half defiantly, half expecting to be laughed at –

> DORA
>
> It'll be two quid . . .

Evidently we have two quid.

She beams with relief – throws her fur over her shoulders, jerks her head towards the right – and sets off . . .

Camera tracks after her . . . Overlaid is the sound of the Man's footsteps . . .

6

Dora resumes her whistling . . . so, under his breath, does the Man who is following her . . .

EXT. A DESERTED STREET. NIGHT

A wider street than the last – but just as empty.

Dora sways her way towards a small house . . . Camera follows at a respectful distance . . .

Camera pans from Dora's hips to an overflowing dustbin.

CLOSE SHOT *of a man's hand throwing something into the dustbin. It is an empty packet marked Kodak Film . . .*

Camera pans to Dora's house . . . It stands next to a chemist shop.

Dora climbs the few steps which lead to her front door – glances round at us encouragingly – then unlocks the door –

INT. HALLWAY OF DORA'S HOUSE. NIGHT

She switches on a light – and hurries up a flight of stairs . . .

Camera tracks after her –

She changes her tune to 'Goodnight Sweetheart' . . . and so – under his breath – does the Man who is following her . . .

A Woman with hair like a two-toned car comes down the stairs, winks at Dora – looks at us for a moment with great curiosity . . . winks . . . then passes out of camera.

Dora reaches the landing – we are close behind her –

INT. LANDING OF DORA'S HOUSE. NIGHT

Dora unlocks the door of her room – and goes inside . . .

INT. DORA'S ROOM. NIGHT

She switches on the light, throws her fur onto a chair, lights the gas fire – then turns round . . .

CLOSE SHOT *of Dora. She holds out her hand – smiling . . .*

And suddenly . . . there is a gentle whirring purring sound –

Camera holds on Dora – she is staring at something with great curiosity –

It turns quickly to bewilderment – and the bewilderment to fear . . .

She steps back from camera – but camera won't have it –

Dora is now staring at something in horror – she opens her mouth to scream – a shadow falls across her face –

The sound purrs on –

    FADE OUT:

    FADE IN:

BLACK AND WHITE FILM SEQUENCE

The solitary figure of Dora standing professionally alone at the end of a street . . . We see her turn towards camera – and smile at us.

We are watching her on a 16mm screen – projected in black and white.

Camera pulls back to show the surround in natural colour.

INT. MARK'S ROOM. NIGHT

A darkened room in natural colour. The movie screen images are in black and white.

We can see the back of a Man's head as he bends intently over a projector . . . He is watching Dora on the screen . . . He is breathing quickly . . .

We see Dora's hips waggling their way home –

The Man raises his head, so that we cannot see the screen . . .

When he lowers it again, we see the Woman with the two-toned hair winking at Dora . . . then we see Dora throwing her fur onto a chair – and turning towards us . . .

We see her staring at something in bewilderment . . . then backing away from camera in fear –

9

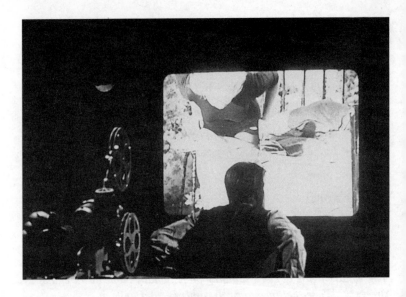

We hear the Man breathing as if at the end of a very long race . . .

*As Dora opens her mouth to scream, and a shadow falls across her face
– the title:*

PEEPING TOM

blots out what is happening to her . . .

*Other credits follow . . . behind them we can see Dora's hands pushing
something away –*

Before the director's credit:

CUT TO:

EXT. A PARK. NIGHT

It is very dark.

CLOSE SHOT *of a stack of deck chairs.*

Two forms behind it – a man's and a woman's . . .

*They are intertwined and motionless . . . suddenly a brilliant shaft of
light is trained onto them . . .*

Overlaid is a gentle, whirring sound . . .

Camera pans quickly to a nearby tree . . .

CLOSE SHOT *of the lens of a cine-camera – the motor purring . . . a blinding spotlight –*

Camera pans to the couple – the whirring of the camera is overlaid.

The Man leaps up – shielding his eyes against the light . . .

He advances towards the tree –

> MAN
> Hey, you peeping –

The spotlight goes out. There is the sound of footsteps running away – and the night is at peace again –

And now we see who directed the picture –

DISSOLVE TO:

LONG SHOT. AMBULANCE. DAY

It is standing in the roadway outside Dora's house.

We see it through the finder of a small cine-camera.

EXT. STREETS BY DORA'S HOUSE. DAY

A crowd has gathered outside the house – and we are watching them from a corner of the street (always through the finder-matte).

We see several Policemen holding back the crowd as two Ambulance Men hurry into the house, carrying an empty stretcher.

A gentle, whirring sound is overlaid –

We see children staring curiously into the empty ambulance – and a group of Women talking excitedly to a Reporter –

CLOSE SHOT *of a small man looking at us curiously as he approaches (filling the screen within the matte).*

> SMALL MAN
> What paper are you from?

II

The finder is lowered.

CLOSE SHOT *of a Young Man (Mark) sighting a cine-camera.*

He lowers the camera – and turns politely to his interrogator.

He seems to have slight difficulty in forming his words.

> MARK

I beg your pardon?

> SMALL MAN

What paper are you from?

Mark smiles at him pleasantly.

> MARK

The Observer –

The Ambulance Men come out of the house carrying the stretcher . . . there is a body on it covered by a sheet . . . Mark raises his cine-camera and photographs them . . . He photographs the ambulance as it drives off . . . He photographs the Policemen dispersing the crowd . . . He photographs his Interrogator, who gladly poses for him . . .

Then he slings his camera over his shoulder, and strolls away . . .

DISSOLVE TO:

CLOSE SHOT *of Dora, smiling happily.*

Her photograph is on the front page of a newspaper.

Above it is a caption: BRUTALLY MURDERED.

Camera pulls back – to show sexy magazines alongside the newspaper.

EXT. A NEWSAGENT'S SHOP. DAY

Mark is staring at a newspaper in the window of a small newsagent's shop.

He glances distastefully at an array of film magazines – showing actresses showing everything – then hurries into the shop.

INT. NEWSAGENT'S SHOP. DAY

A plump, bald-headed Man stares at Mark.

                    MR PETERS
You're late –

                    MARK
Sorry, sir –

He turns towards a small door at the end of the shop.

                    MR PETERS
                    (*quietly*)
Hold on, Mark –

Mark turns round –

Mr Peters hesitates, drumming his fingers on the counter.

CLOSE SHOT *of Mark. He starts to drum his fingers on a shelf.*

Mark . . . I've a question for you –

He stops drumming his fingers.

So, at that moment, does Mark.

Which magazines sell the most copies?

                    MARK
Those with girls on the front covers – and no front covers on
the girls –

                    MR PETERS
Exactly! . . . And it's just the same with the work you do for
me –

Overlaid is the sound of the door opening.

Look busy –

Mark busies himself sorting some newspapers.

A whole row of Doras smile up at him . . .

Camera pans to doorway of the shop.

An Elderly Gentleman is standing there.

ELDERLY GENTLEMAN

The Times, please –

MR PETERS

Certainly, sir –

ELDERLY GENTLEMAN

And *The Telegraph* –

MR PETERS

Certainly, sir – anything else?

The Elderly Gentleman hesitates – glancing at Mark's back.

Then:

ELDERLY GENTLEMAN

I . . . er . . . have been told by a friend that you . . . er . . . have some views for sale?

MR PETERS

What sort of views, sir?

ELDERLY GENTLEMAN

Well – er –

MR PETERS

This sort, sir?

From under the counter he produces a thick book.

Mark turns round.

From his POV we see the Elderly Gentleman open the book.

He – er – seems – er – more than a little interested.

ELDERLY GENTLEMAN

I – er . . . how much each?

MR PETERS

Five shillings, sir.

ELDERLY GENTLEMAN

I'll take this one . . . and – er . . . this one . . . and – er . . . how much would the lot be?

MR PETERS

To you – five pounds, sir . . .

The Elderly Gentleman hesitates.

Mr Peters turns over a page . . . and the Elderly Gentleman almost turns over with it.

Tell you what, sir. Four pounds ten – and I'll throw in *The Times* and *Telegraph* . . . how's that?

ELDERLY GENTLEMAN

Well, er . . . thank you very much –

MR PETERS

Let me wrap it for you, sir –

He puts it in a wrapper which says 'Educational Books'.

– shall I put you on our mailing list?

ELDERLY GENTLEMAN

Oh no! But I'll look in again . . .

MR PETERS

By all means, sir.

He holds open the door for the Elderly Gentleman, and watches him leave.

He won't be doing the crossword tonight!

He turns triumphantly to Mark.

> (*counting out money from wallet*)
> Those pictures he chose . . . were all yours!
> (*handing notes*)
> This is yours!

Mark pockets them without counting them.

CLOSE SHOT *of Mark.*

> MR PETERS
> (*in a very different tone*)
> And this is yours too . . .

He picks up a postcard – holds it towards Mark.

> And that's what I want to talk to you about. It's a clever picture – because you're a clever lad . . . but, Mark . . .
> (*pathetically*)
> It's all face –

Mark looks at the postcard in silence.

> I don't want to hurt your feelings, son – but if people want the *Mona Lisa* they go to the National Gallery –

> MARK
> The Louvre –

> MR PETERS
> Well, wherever they go, they don't come here . . . so no more of this fancy stuff –

He pats Mark's arm.

> – now get upstairs – the girls are waiting . . . and so is a bonus if you give me what I want –

> MARK
> Thank you, sir –

MR PETERS
(*amused*)
What do you do with all your money?

MARK
Buy cameras –

He opens a door at the far end of the room. We catch a glimpse of a winding staircase. He starts to climb it.

INT. REAR OF NEWSAGENT'S SHOP. DAY

At the top of the staircase is a door. Mark and his camera trudge towards it. The door opens suddenly. A vivacious young redhead – Milly – pokes her head round . . . She has a towel round her shoulders . . .

MILLY
Well look who's here! Cecil Beaton!

From reverse angle we see Mark venture a shy smile at Milly . . . Milly opens the door impatiently.

Come on, sonny . . . make us famous –

Through the half-open door we catch a glimpse of a second girl (Lorraine) . . . She is staring out of a window, her back to camera . . . She is naked except for a shawl draped round her shoulders.

Mark enters the room . . . the door begins to close. Camera tracks towards the door. On the threshold of the room, a hood is thrown over our faces . . . the screen blacks out.

In the darkness we hear Milly's voice –

(*off-screen*)
Did you read about that girl who was murdered last night?

INT. STUDIO ABOVE NEWSAGENT'S. DAY

We are with Mark under the hood of an antiquated camera. Through the ground-glass of the camera we see a small inverted image of Milly . . .

MILLY
(*off-screen*)
The same thing nearly happened to me!

We hear Lorraine's voice – muffled, and very far away.

LORRAINE
(*off-screen*)

When?

MILLY
(*off-screen*)
Last night! I went out with my boyfriend . . . We're getting married next month . . . trouble was my fiancé saw us –

The small inverted image of Milly peers anxiously into the camera.

– can you fix it so the bruises don't show?

The ground-glass camera begins travelling slowly down Milly's back –

CLOSE SHOT *of Milly. She is on a couch, lying on her stomach at a slightly oblique angle. All that we can see are her face and naked shoulders.*

From Milly's POV we see Mark under the hood of an antiquated camera.

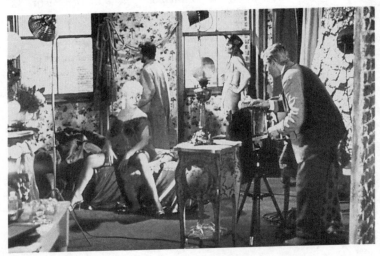

Well, can you?

Mark's voice is muffled under the hood.

MARK

I think so, Milly –

MILLY

Then be quick about it, sonny! I'm freezing.

CLOSE SHOT *of her naked toes. They start to wriggle.*

CLOSE SHOT *of Mark's toes – in sandals, next to the tripod of the camera . . . They start to wriggle . . .*

CLOSE SHOT *of Lorraine. We watch her in profile as she stares out of the window – clutching her shawl. She has outstandingly beautiful features . . .*

CLOSE SHOT *of Mark. He is standing by the side of the camera, studying us thoughtfully . . . He is holding a remote-control switch panel in his hand . . . He clicks off several lights and then switches several others on . . . then he ducks back under the hood.*

There he goes again! What have you got under there? A girlfriend?

We join Mark under the hood.

We see a small inverted image of Milly on the ground-glass . . . Her shoulders are now white and glistening, her spine caressed by shadows . . . She is staring into the camera.

I suppose you *have* a girlfriend?

He adjusts the focus. We can see more clearly the contempt on Milly's face.

MARK

No, Milly –

MILLY

Hear that, Lorraine? He's available –

19

From Milly's POV we see Mark come round to the front of the camera, and insert a dark slide.

MARK

Raise your head, please – and look at the sea –

MILLY
(off-screen)

What sea?

Mark presses a rubber bulb – the shutter clicks.

What sea?

Mark inserts another dark slide.

MARK

I just wanted that puzzled look –

MILLY
(off-screen)

Oh, did you? Well if you want it again, I'll think of you –

Camera pulls back –

From Milly's viewpoint, we see Mark holding the rubber bulb . . . His cine-camera is on a ledge behind him.

    You're a puzzle and a half.

Mark presses the rubber bulb – the shutters click.

    This is a spare time job for you, isn't it?

MARK

    Yes, Milly.

He inserts another slide.

MILLY

    Well, what do you do for a living?

MARK

    Take pictures –

He presses the bulb – the shutters click.

MILLY

    This sort?

MARK

    No, Milly –

He inserts another slide.

MILLY

    Don't you like this sort?

MARK

    No, Milly –

He presses the bulb – the shutters click.

MILLY

    Well what sort do you like?

Mark looks at her thoughtfully for a long moment.

MARK

    I may show you – one day –

That'll be a treat, I'm sure –

Mark smiles at her shyly.

MARK

That's all, Milly –

MILLY

Oh no, sonny! Now take one I can show my mother!

Mark inserts another slide.

MARK

Think of her then –

There is a gentle knock at the door, and Mr Peters enters. He carries a tray of coffee. He keeps his eyes modestly lowered.

MR PETERS

On the house –

He lays the tray on a table, still keeping his eyes lowered, and goes out.

MILLY

Some house! Hope it falls on his ruddy earhole –

She glances over her shoulder.

It's your turn now, love –

CLOSE SHOT *of Lorraine staring out of the window . . . She stiffens . . . Milly's voice is overlaid.*

(*off-screen, in a whisper*)
– it's her first time –

Lorraine clutches her shawl tightly . . .

Come on, love. Don't be shy –

Lorraine turns round.

The left side of her face is classical in its beauty. She has a hare lip, which twists and distorts the whole of the right side . . . Her eyes are large – and beautiful – and defiant . . .

CLOSE SHOT *of Mark looking at her.*

CLOSE SHOT *of Lorraine.*

> **LORRAINE**
> He said . . . you needn't photograph my face –

CLOSE SHOT *of Mark.*

> **MARK**
> I want to –

CLOSE SHOT *of Lorraine. Beautiful in profile.*

> **LORRAINE**
> I suppose you'll fix *my* bruises too?

> **MARK**
> I want to . . .

> **MILLY**
> What about the customers?

CLOSE SHOT *of the shawl round Lorraine's shoulders . . .*

CLOSE SHOT *of Mark.*

> **MARK**
> You needn't be shy . . . of me . . . it's my first time too –

CLOSE SHOT *of Lorraine's eyes – puzzled.*

> **LORRAINE**
> Yours?

> **MARK**
> In front of eyes . . . like . . .

He tries to go on – but words are a foreign language to him . . .

> . . . eyes . . . as full of . . .

In a sudden rush:

> Lorraine – let my camera tell you –

CLOSE SHOT *of Lorraine standing very still – looking at him in silence.*

Milly shrugs and reaches for the coffee pot.

Overlaid is the gentle purring of a cine-camera . . .

23

Camera lingers on the dark liquid being poured into a cup . . .

DISSOLVE TO:

Whisky being poured into a glass . . .

Camera pulls back –

INT. HELEN'S SITTING ROOM. EVENING. TOWARDS SUNSET

The hand filling the glass is a woman's (Mrs Stephens). She is sitting in a high-backed chair, and we cannot see her face. Over her shoulder we watch a party in progress. A group of young people have surrounded someone to whom they are singing:

> Happy birthday to you –
> Happy birthday to you –

Camera tracks towards them . . .

CLOSE SHOT *of Tony Hunter, a well-built youngster in his middle twenties.*

TONY
Happy birthday . . . dear Helen –

He obviously means it –

– happy birthday to you –

CLOSE SHOT *of 'dear Helen'. A sensitive, intelligent, and extremely attractive girl, who – as the encircling youngsters now inform us in song – is:*

> Twenty-one today –
> She's twenty-one today –
> She's got the key of the door –
> She's never been twenty-one before –

CLOSE SHOT *of the glass by Mrs Stephens' side. It is half empty . . . An elderly lady leans across to her . . . She is Mrs Partridge, slightly high on a glass of sherry . . .*

MRS PARTRIDGE
You must be very proud of your daughter, Mrs Stephens.

Mrs Stephens grunts . . . Someone switches on a gramophone and the young couples start dancing at once. Tony hurries up to Helen.

> TONY

May I?

Helen goes towards him. A Young Man calls out sharply:

> YOUNG MAN

Look!

He is pointing at something out of camera . . . All heads – except Mrs Stephens' – follow the direction of his gaze . . . Mrs Stephens continues to sit motionless in the high-backed chair.

Camera pans to the window. Mark is standing there.

CLOSE SHOT *of Helen looking at Mark. We watch him over her shoulder – Tony's arm encircling it.*

> TONY
> (*off-screen*)

It's that chap from upstairs –

EXT. MARK'S HOUSE. EVENING. LOW SUN

The chap from upstairs presses his face to the window. From his POV we see Helen's eyes looking at him – the key of the door in them – looking at him, not staring . . . Suddenly the rest comes into focus – Tony's arm around Helen's shoulder . . . the high-backed chair in the foreground with the back of that motionless head . . . a young couple giggling as they stare at him. Mark steps away, and the camera pulls back with him . . .

We catch a glimpse of the house – large, sprawling, but with a touch of quality about it, in a quiet, unpretentious street.

Mark hurries towards a side entrance.

INT. HELEN'S SITTING ROOM. EVENING

CLOSE SHOT *of Helen looking at the empty window.*

> HELEN

I'll ask him in –

CLOSE SHOT *of Tony – frowning* . . .

Camera pans to Mrs Stephens' glass . . . the hand which refills it has begun to tremble . . .

INT. REAR OF HOUSE. NIGHT

The lights are on.

We follow Mark (and his camera) along a small passage which leads to the hall . . . The sound of a dance record can be heard . . . Mark starts to whistle it under his breath . . .

INT. HALL. NIGHT

Over his shoulder we see a staircase, and beyond it the door of Helen's sitting room . . . The sound of Helen's party fills the hall . . .

Mark reaches the staircase . . . There is the sound of a door opening . . . Helen's voice is overlaid:

> HELEN
> (*off-screen*)

Excuse me –

Mark hesitates, then turns round.

CLOSE SHOT *of Helen – smiling at him.*

I don't know how many times we've passed each other on the stairs –

Mark looks at her as if he does.

– but tonight I'm determined at least to say hallo to you! So hallo!

Her directness is natural, consistent and very hard to resist.

CLOSE SHOT *of Mark – smiling.*

I'm Helen Stephens –

She glances with unconcealed interest at the camera over his shoulder.

I'm having a party – and the other tenants are there . . . and a few friends. We'd like you to join us.

MARK

Mark –

HELEN

Pardon?

MARK

I'm Mark –

HELEN

Hallo, Mark –

She holds out her hand . . . he takes it gently.

Please come in . . . you'll meet the others who live here,
and –

MARK

Thank you, but . . . work –

HELEN

Oh . . .

She glances again at his camera.

Well, I hope to keep it going for hours yet . . . so when you've
finished why not look in?

She realizes that this is not the happiest of phrases.

– Mark?

He hesitates.

Camera pans to Helen's door. Tony stands there.

TONY

Darling, your cake – everyone's waiting –

CLOSE SHOT *of Mark.*

Looking at her.

MARK

Thank you –

He turns away.

27

– happy birthday –

He hurries up the stairs . . .

CLOSE SHOT *of Helen. She stares after him for a moment . . . Then returns thoughtfully to her party . . .*

FADE OUT:

The screen remains dark for a moment. We are with Mark in a darkened room. He is giving a film show – and we are the screen . . .

INT. MARK'S DARK-ROOM. NIGHT

His cine-projector points straight at us . . . A flickering light shines in our eyes. We can see him crouching behind the projector.

Mark leans forward, watching the screen intently . . . perspiration trickles down his forehead . . . He is breathing very quickly . . . The sounds of the party seep up from downstairs – music, laughter, and a girl's yelp . . .

There is a knock on the door. Mark does not hear it.

Camera pans to the door of the room . . . It is blacked-out like a photographic dark-room . . . The knock is repeated.

CLOSE SHOT *of Mark. He switches off the projector instantly . . .*

Camera pans to an open cupboard in the corner . . .

CLOSE SHOT *of the shelves. They are stacked with spools of film . . .*

Camera travels slowly over these spools. We see Mark's hand add two more to the collection; his voice is overlaid.

> MARK
> (*off-screen*)

– minute –

He closes the cupboard door . . .

INT. MARK'S SITTING ROOM. NIGHT

Mark comes out of the dark-room behind him – the light is kept out by a baffle and a curtain. He has a pleasant, normally untidy bedsitting room . . .

*He wipes his handkerchief across his forehead – then hurries to the door.
He opens it – Helen is standing there . . .*

HELEN

I hope I'm not disturbing you –

CLOSE SHOT *of Mark – shaking his head, smiling shyly . . .*

CLOSE SHOT *of Helen.*

I knew you wouldn't come down . . . so I've brought you
this –

She holds out a plate on which is a piece of birthday cake.

MARK

Thank you –

He takes the plate.

– very much . . .

HELEN

I mustn't keep you from your work –

She turns to go . . .

                         MARK
         I'd like to offer you a drink –

She turns round.

                         HELEN
         Thank you, Mark –

                         MARK
         I haven't one –

                         HELEN
         I'd adore some water –

She smiles.

         – a hostess can't drink water at her own party, it looks like a
         hint to the guests –

                         MARK
         Will you . . . would you . . . like to come in?

                         HELEN
         Yes, Mark . . .

She steps over the threshold . . . The door closes behind her . . .

INT. MARK'S SITTING ROOM. NIGHT

CLOSE SHOT *of Helen looking round the room . . .*

Mark's voice is overlaid.

                         MARK
                      (*off-screen*)
         There's milk . . . if you'd like some –

                         HELEN
         Very much . . . if you can spare it –

                         MARK
                      (*off-screen*)
         Yes –

Helen glances towards the inner room . . . He holds out a glass of milk
to her.

HELEN

Thank you, Mark . . .

She drinks it with relish. He watches her in silence.

This is a pleasant room . . . and you've another inside?

MARK

Yes.

HELEN

How long have you lived here?

MARK

All my life –

She looks at him in surprise.

I was born in this house –

HELEN

Oh?

CLOSE SHOT *of Mark.*

MARK

It's my father's –

HELEN

Do you mean I've at last found out who our landlord is? Your father?

MARK

Well – no . . . he's dead –

He hesitates.

I'm the landlord.

She looks at him in astonishment.

HELEN

YOU?

MARK

Yes –

HELEN

But you walk about as if you haven't paid the rent –

MARK

I haven't.

HELEN

I meant –

MARK

I know –

CLOSE SHOT *of Mark.*

It's his house – and I'll never sell it . . . but I can't afford the upkeep, so I let rooms –

He looks at her anxiously.

– if I charge too much, tell me and I'll tell the agents.

HELEN

The rent's very reasonable, but don't say anything to the others or you'll have no peace –

MARK
(*slowly*)

Peace . . . ?

CLOSE SHOT *of Helen.*

HELEN

Mark, what do you do?

MARK

Most of the time, I work in a film studio –

HELEN

On the photographic side, I'll bet –

MARK

I hope to be a film director . . . very soon –

HELEN

How exciting.

MARK

I have some spare time jobs . . . as well –

HELEN

To do with photography?

MARK

More milk?

HELEN

No thank you . . . to do with photography?

MARK

Yes . . . to do with photography . . .

HELEN

When I came in were you looking at some films?

MARK

Yes –

HELEN

Of yours?

MARK

Yes –

HELEN

I'd like to see them . . .

He looks at her in silence.

I know I'm being rude . . . but I really would like to see
them –

She smiles.

– it would be a birthday present . . . from you to me . . .

MARK

Would it?

HELEN

Yes, Mark.

MARK

Oh . . .

HELEN

But I suppose you're too busy –

She puts down the glass, turns to the door.

MARK

Will you . . . would you . . . like to see them now?

She turns round. He is standing by the entrance to the inner room . . .

HELEN

Thank you . . .

MARK

I'll – go first –

He leads the way – she follows.

For a moment the screen is in darkness. A dark-room darkness.

INT. THE INNER ROOM. NIGHT

We can hear – faintly – the dance music from downstairs.

There is a click – and the walls are suddenly bathed in diffused light, throwing the room into delicate shadow . . .

CLOSE SHOT *of Helen looking round in amazement.*

As certain events of possible interest are to take place in this room, here, in detail, is what amazes Helen . . .

The room is the product of three rooms which have been knocked into one. It is very large and extremely well constructed (as we are soon to learn, it was originally a laboratory). One half of the room is used for processing, and the other half for filming – and for trade shows. The two halves are lined by long shelves upon which are perched all shapes and sizes of cameras, their spectacles glinting in the light.

In the processing half two benches (a 'dry' bench and a 'wet' bench) face each other against opposite walls. There are three sinks above the 'wet' bench and an outburst of equipment above the 'dry'.

This part of the room is lit by two dark-room lamps frowning in the ceiling above the benches.

The other part of the room has a window at the far end of it. Heavy drapes are pulled across it.

Mark's projector rests on a small table in front of the 16mm screen.

Two banks of floods and a variety of spots light this part of the room. There is a small control panel on the wall.

Some of the equipment is ancient – but none of it is old. All of it glistens with the affection of its owner.

There is absolutely nothing in the room to alarm anyone except an adult . . . the kind who starts to wonder who paid for it all.

CLOSE SHOT *of Mark. He stands by the lighting panel, watching Helen.*

From his POV we see her brushing the hair out of her eyes as she looks slowly round. He brushes the hair out of his . . . For a moment she turns her back to him. He presses a switch on the wall . . . A gentle light ripples through the back of Helen's hair . . .

CLOSE SHOT *of Helen. She turns to him . . . She is very nearly at a loss for words.*

HELEN

This is so . . . well – so many things . . . but above all – it's
so –

She takes a final look round.

. . . completely unexpected!

She looks at him searchingly.

Is all of it yours?

MARK

Yes.

HELEN

I mean . . . is it designed by you? Furnished by you? Tell me
about this room –

CLOSE SHOT *of Mark.*

MARK

It belonged to my father –

HELEN

What was he?

MARK

Scientist . . .

HELEN

Then this equipment was his?

MARK

No . . .

He hesitates.

I sold his to buy it –

HELEN

But it seems to be so – technical –

She looks at him with renewed interest.

If this is where you work, I can't wait to see what you work
at –

CLOSE SHOT *of Mark – in difficulties.*

>   MARK
>   Don't know what to show you –

>   HELEN
>   Well . . . what were you looking at when I interrupted you?

He looks at her thoughtfully . . .

>   MARK
>   All right!

He crosses to the corner cupboard – opens the door –

CLOSE SHOT *of the cupboard.*

We see Mark's hand reach for a spool of film . . . then hesitate, poised above another spool.

CLOSE SHOT *of Helen – watching with interest.*

REVERSE ANGLE SHOT *of Mark. He closes the cupboard, and turns round . . . there is a spool of film in his hand –*

He walks slowly towards his projector . . . he seems – for the moment – to have forgotten she is there . . .

CLOSE SHOT *of Helen – watching him thread the film into the projector.*

>   This is the first . . . twenty-first birthday present . . . I'll ever
>   have given –

>   HELEN
>   It's the first I've ever asked for . . .

He places a chair a few feet away from the screen – and, with an oddly courteous bow, beckons her into it. She sits down.

CLOSE SHOT *of Mark. He looks at her intently for a moment – then turns off the lights . . . Over Helen's shoulder we can just make out the empty screen . . . Mark switches on the projector . . .*

CLOSE SHOT *of Helen – the light flickering on her face.*

CLOSE SHOT *of Mark staring at Helen's face.*

CLOSE SHOT *of Helen. We see her expression of surprise. Over Mark's shoulder we see the surprise growing . . . Over Helen's shoulder we see the screen . . . We are looking at a small boy. He is lying in his bed asleep . . . Although the print is old, we can see that he is a remarkably handsome boy . . .*

HELEN

Mark – what a beautiful child –

The boy turns restlessly in his sleep . . . one of his pillows falls to the floor . . .

Who is he?

MARK
(*quietly*)

Me –

HELEN

Of course it is! . . . Then who took this film?

MARK

My father –

*A light – as if from a small torch – starts to shine on the child's eyes . . .
He moves restlessly . . .*

HELEN

What a wonderful idea . . .

*The light plays on the child's left eye, then on his right . . . It is growing
brighter.*

– you'll be able to show it to your own chi–

*The child wakes up suddenly . . . He stares at something . . . then starts
to scream –*

You must have had a bad dream . . .

CLOSE SHOT *of Mark watching her in silence.*

. . . but what was that light? . . . The camera, I suppose?

*Mark does not answer. The small screen is filled with the face of the
screaming, terrified child . . .*

(Mark's father now tries a not altogether successful dissolve:)

*We now see the little boy standing in front of a garden wall . . . He tries
hard to climb to the top of the wall, but falls over . . . Helen laughs . . .
Mark watches her in silence . . . Small Mark tries again – and again –
to scale the wall . . . at last he succeeds . . .*

Whatever are you after?

*We see the little boy lying flat on the wall staring at something . . . rapt,
motionless.*

*The cine-camera which is taking this picture now tracks rather clumsily
towards the wall . . .*

High angle shot over the wall of what is fascinating young Mark –

A man and woman are lying on the ground, kissing . . .

*The cine-camera pans – again rather clumsily – to young Mark . . .
staring intently . . .*

Naughty boy – I hope you were spanked!

CLOSE SHOT *of Helen. It suddenly occurs to her.*

> – but, Mark . . . what a strange thing for your father to
> photograph –

MARK

Switch off?

HELEN

No –

She stares again at that lonely figure perched on the wall.

No –

The small screen begins to dissolve . . . so does the large.

DISSOLVE TO:

INT. HELEN'S SITTING ROOM. NIGHT

*Over Mrs Stephens' shoulder we see the party in progress. The glass by
her side is full again. Tony is dancing with an attractive blonde.*

MRS STEPHENS

Tony!

He turns round.

TONY

Me, Mrs Stephens?

The head nods.

Tony advances reluctantly towards her . . .

Reverse angle shot of Mrs Stephens.

Over Tony's shoulder we see a powerfully built and once lovely woman.

*She is so perpetually drunk as almost to be sober. The few movements
she makes are slow – deliberate – and give nothing away. The voice
articulates so carefully that the slur scarcely shows . . .*

The fact that she is blind almost helps to conceal the fact that she is drunk . . . Her sightless eyes stare out the camera as Tony reaches her . . .

MRS STEPHENS

I want a word with you –

DISSOLVE TO:

CLOSE SHOT *of Helen's eyes. The light from the projector flickering into them . . .*

HELEN

I hate people who chatter in films – but there's so much I want to ask –

Camera pulls back.

INT. THE INNER ROOM. NIGHT

She is leaning forward, her face cupped in her hand, watching the small screen intently . . .

CLOSE SHOT *of Mark. His face is cupped in his hand as he watches her intently . . .*

Over Helen's shoulder we see Mark in the making –

The child is again asleep . . . this time he is being photographed from the head of the bed – the camera pointing straight down at his face.

A beam of light starts to shine onto his eyes, first onto the left, then onto the right . . .

HELEN
(in a whisper)

Again?

Mark looks at her in silence.

The boy moves restlessly, then turns over onto his face, pulling the bedclothes round him . . . His right hand is limp on the pillow . . . The light shines for a moment on this hand, then goes out . . .

Helen half turns towards Mark.

41

Mark – this isn't some sort of jo–

Her attention is suddenly riveted on the screen.

> MARK
> (*in a whisper*)

No, Helen.

Over Helen's shoulder we see something drop onto the child's bed . . . something which stays quite still for a moment, then starts crawling towards the counterpane . . . It is a small lizard.

> HELEN

Mark – whatever – is that?

Her voice trails away . . . She stares – repelled and fascinated – at the screen . . .

We see Mark reach for his cine-camera . . .

Over Helen's shoulder we see the lizard reach the counterpane. It stretches itself out on the floral design – its body is pointed towards the child's hand . . .

We hear a click – and suddenly a spotlight falls onto Helen's face . . .

Overlaid is the gentle purring of Mark's cine-camera.

She wheels towards him – blotting out the small screen.

What are you –

> MARK

. . . wanted to photograph you . . . watching –

> HELEN

No, Mark –

The camera purrs on.

– no –

He switches off the spot . . . the purring of the camera dies away. She turns towards the small screen . . .

– help me to understand this . . . this nightmare . . .

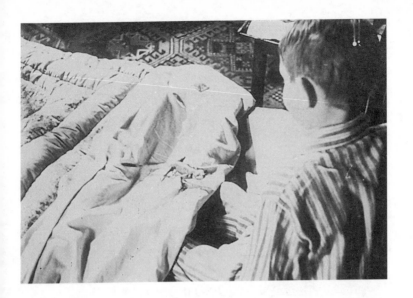

The small boy is sitting upright . . . screaming with terror . . . there is no sign of the lizard . . .

A handkerchief is thrown onto the boy's bed. He continues crying – looking up into someone's face . . .

CLOSE SHOT *of Mark watching the screen . . .*

We hear a man's deep voice overlaid.

(off-screen)
That'll do Mark . . . dry your eyes and stop being silly –

Small Mark reaches for the handkerchief and wipes his eyes . . . his hands are trembling –

The small screen trembles with them into a clumsy dissolve –

Helen turns to Mark.

HELEN
All right . . . now look . . . Mark – what was all that about?

He looks at her helplessly . . .

– that was a lizard, wasn't it? Or a –

MARK

– liz –

HELEN

Well how did it get there? . . . How did it get there Mark? . . .
Was it a pet?

MARK

Not mine –

HELEN

Won't you try to explain?

CLOSE SHOT *of Mark staring at the screen.*

MARK

You'd better go –

HELEN

I like to understand what I'm shown!

She turns to the screen –

What was your father trying to do? . . . Photographing you at
nigh–

Her voice trails away.

MARK

– better go –

From Helen's POV we see the screen . . .

Small Mark is wearing a dark suit and a black tie.

*He is standing at the foot of a four-poster bed, staring at something in
horror and disbelief . . . his hands clasp the bedrail tightly . . .*

*Slowly – very slowly – he walks towards the head of the bed,
staring . . .*

*His lips begin to quiver . . . He bends forward over the bed . . . We can
see the back of his bowed head . . .*

44

HELEN

Mark . . . what is this?

MARK

I am saying . . . goodbye . . . my mother . . .

We catch a glimpse of a woman's hands folded in front of her.

CLOSE SHOT *of Helen.*

HELEN
(in a whisper)
He . . . photographed . . . that . . .?

CLOSE SHOT *of Mark.*

MARK

Yes –

Suddenly – and healthily – his temper snaps.

– and this –

He pushes a lever on his projector as far forward as it will go –

The film is now shown at tremendous speed –

We catch a glimpse of a long line of cars . . .

– her funeral –

It speeds by.

– and this –

A confused picture of earth and flowers.

– her burial –

The briefest glimpse of a little boy with a spade.

– and this –

We see a girl in a bikini by sand-dunes.

Mark offers no comment.

HELEN

Mark – who is that?

MARK

Her successor –

CLOSE SHOT *of Helen.*

HELEN

Suc–?

MARK

He married her . . . six weeks after . . . the previous
sequence –

*He pulls back the lever of his projector . . . the film returns to its normal
speed.*

*We see the same attractive young woman standing in a garden . . . She
is holding a bewildered and defiant Mark by the hand.*

Suddenly the girl runs towards camera – leaving Mark standing alone.

She filmed . . . what comes now –

CLOSE SHOT *of Helen watching intently.*

It's out of focus!

*From Helen's POV we see a tall man in a black coat walking away
from camera. He hurries towards small Mark – who watches him
anxiously . . .*

HELEN

Is that your father?

MARK

The morning that he left for his honeymoon –

*The back of Mark's father suddenly obscures our view of small Mark
. . . all we can see is that tall figure looking downwards standing very
still . . .*

Camera wobbles – as if the person holding it is laughing . . .

HELEN

What is he doing?

MARK

Giving me a present . . .

HELEN

What was it?

Mark stares at the blurred screen, perspiration trickling down his forehead.

MARK

Can't you guess?

The small screen comes back into focus – and suddenly our camera rushes towards it . . .

We see a CLOSE SHOT *of a* CLOSE SHOT *– and at the moment we see it, Mark's voice is overlaid . . . a whisper which echoes round the room.*

(off-screen)

A camera –

We are looking at a close shot of a camera in a small boy's hands.

There is a single shrill chord of music on the sound track.

CLOSE SHOT *of the shelf which encircles Mark's room.*

We are looking at the very same camera which the small boy is holding.

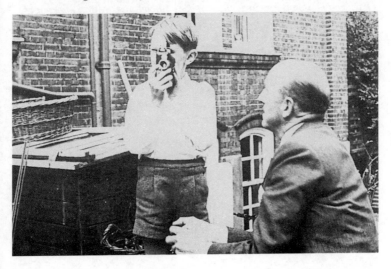

CLOSE SHOT *of the camera in small Mark's hands.*

His father's finger points to the view-finder . . .

Small Mark stares into it . . . Small Mark begins to smile –

CLOSE SHOT *of Mark watching himself being born.*

CLOSE SHOT *of Helen watching Mark.*

> HELEN
>
> Switch it off –

He continues to stare at the screen . . .

> Switch it off, Mark –

She turns to the projector – touches the wrong switch . . .

Small Mark and his father go rapidly backwards . . .

Mark turns off the projector abruptly.

The room is in darkness –

We can hear both of them breathing quickly . . .

The light goes on . . . Mark is standing by the exit – he keeps his face averted –

Helen walks slowly towards the exit . . . She glances round once, over her shoulder, then goes into the other room . . .

Mark stares after her.

INT. MARK'S SITTING ROOM. NIGHT

She walks towards the door . . . turns round suddenly – almost in anger.

> HELEN
>
> So he was a scientist?

He keeps his face averted.

> What kind of scientist, Mark?

> MARK
>
> Biologist.

What was he trying to do to you?

He doesn't answer.

Mark! . . .

He turns round slowly.

From his POV we see the willingness to understand on her face.

What was he trying to do to you?

MARK

Watch me . . . grow up . . .

She walks towards him . . . takes his handkerchief from his jacket pocket and wipes his forehead.

He wanted a record of a growing child . . . complete in every detail – if such a thing were possible – and he tried to make it possible by training a camera on me . . . at all times . . .

CLOSE SHOT *of Mark.*

I never knew . . . the whole of my childhood . . . one moment's privacy . . .

HELEN

And those lights in your eyes? . . . and that – thing?

MARK

He was interested . . . in the reactions of the nervous system . . . to fear . . .

HELEN

Fear?

MARK

Fear –

CLOSE SHOT *of the word 'fear'.*

Camera pulls back –

We are looking at the spine of a book on Mark's shelf. The full title reads: The Physiology of Fear *by Professor A. N. Lewis.*

Mark's voice is overlaid:

Especially fear in children – and how they react to it –

CLOSE SHOT *of the word 'fear' on the next book* . . .

Camera pulls back –

The full title reads: Fear and the Nervous System, Part I. *Professor A. N. Lewis.*

There is a row of such books all by Professor Lewis.

CLOSE SHOT *of Mark.*

I think he learned a lot . . . from me . . . I'd wake up . . . screaming . . . sometimes . . . and he'd be there . . . taking notes . . . and pictures . . . and I'm sure good came of it . . . for some people . . . He was brilliant –

HELEN

A scientist drops a lizard onto a child's bed – and good comes of it?

MARK

I don't know . . . if he did . . . but if he did . . . he'll have learned something of value . . .

HELEN

If only about lizards! Mark – it sounds to me as if your father was –

MARK

He founded clinics –

HELEN

He sounds completely –

MARK

He was famous! Professor A. N. Lewis . . . three clinics –

HELEN

Why do you still live in his house . . . and watch his films?

MARK

They helped make me . . . what I am –

HELEN

A photographer? It's no wonder, is it? But you still haven't
shown me anything *you've* photographed!

He looks at her in silence.

Will you?

There is a knock on the door.

MARK

One day –

He hurries to the door, and opens it.

Tony is standing there –

TONY

Excuse me, but –

*From Tony's POV we see Helen looking at the door of the dark
room . . .*

Oh, there you are, Helen.

She turns towards him.

The party looks like breaking up, and we were wondering if –

HELEN

I'm coming –

She turns to Mark.

I wish you'd join us –

Mark shakes his head.

MARK

Thanks . . . work –

HELEN

I hope that you –

*She is suddenly aware of Tony watching her . . . She glances at the
birthday cake on the table.*

– have a sweet tooth!

51

She smiles at him.

Thank you . . . for my present –

She goes into the passage.

TONY

Good night, old boy –

He puts his arm round Helen, and closes the door.

Mark stares after them, motionless.

The camera lingers on the birthday cake . . .

As the light fades, a voice yells:

Cut!

INT. FILM STUDIO. DAY

HIGH ANGLE *shot of a set showing part of a large West End store.*

A blonde is lying unconscious in front of a lift – and a crowd of extras surround her.

As the word 'cut' dies away, the extras relax – and the blonde (Diane Ashley) props herself onto her elbow, looking towards the Director.

CLOSE SHOT *of the Director (Arthur Baden) standing beside the camera.*

BADEN

OK. Print that one!

He glances at the Chief Cameraman (Philip Tate), who nods his head in agreement.

CLOSE SHOT *of Mark standing at the back of the camera crew. He shakes his head in disagreement.*

The Chief Cameraman spots Mark's small mutiny and wags his finger at him. As the Chief Cameraman turns away, Mark's finger automatically wags back . . .

CLOSE SHOT *of Baden looking at his watch. He sighs, then nods to the Assistant Director who stands beside him.*

All right, everyone! Back at two!

Baden walks out without a word to anyone. A hubbub of chatter breaks out. The unit downs tools and begins to disperse.

CLOSE SHOT *of one of the extras (Vivian) – a small, vivacious, brunette with delicate, attractive features.*

She edges towards the camera crew.

CLOSE SHOT *of Mark watching her . . .*

Over his shoulder we see Vivian glance towards him . . . He nods almost imperceptibly.

Vivian hurries towards the exit.

Mark turns to a shelf behind him – picks up his cine-camera and a little full string bag containing his lunch.

DISSOLVE TO:

EXT. STUDIO GROUNDS. DAY

CLOSE SHOT *of Vivian munching a sandwich.*

Camera pulls back.

She is leaning against a wall in a corner of an exterior set – a Chinese temple or a medieval castle (or a combination of each like a Pinewood drawing-room).

Beside her she has a small tape-recorder, or record-player. We hear music – modern rhythms.

There are several people strolling about – but no one in the immediate vicinity. No one . . . except Mark.

CLOSE SHOT *of Mark – settling down on the other side of the wall (where they can talk without being seen together).*

VIVIAN

Mark?

MARK

Hallo . . .

VIVIAN

Were you spotted?

MARK

Don't think so.

VIVIAN
(*switches off music*)

Is it . . . tonight?

CLOSE SHOT *of Mark.*

MARK

Yes –

CLOSE SHOT *of Vivian.*

VIVIAN

Mark . . .

MARK

Yes?

VIVIAN

You're sure we won't be caught?

MARK

Not if you do as I tell you –

VIVIAN

I will, I promise –

MARK

You haven't . . . said anything . . . to anyone?

VIVIAN

Of course not –

MARK

Good . . . like some cake?

VIVIAN

Thank you –

We see him break off a piece of birthday cake, and pass it over to her.

Mark . . . I want to be quite clear about this . . .

CLOSE SHOT *of Mark staring at his cake.*

Tonight, when the studio's empty . . . I'm to come back – and you're going to give me a film test . . . right?

>   MARK
> Right.

>   VIVIAN
> You'll then print the film – so I can show it to my agent and anyone else who matters – right?

>   MARK
> Right –

>   VIVIAN
> Mark –

She hesitates.

– I've been offered film tests before . . . but I haven't liked the terms.

>   MARK
> There aren't any –

>   VIVIAN
> Then why are you doing this? Risking your job and –

>   MARK
> Not just for you . . . Viv . . . I have an agent too – and I want to show him what *I* can do . . . I want to direct . . .

>   VIVIAN
>   (*switching on music again*)
> There's someone coming –

Mark lies motionless behind the wall. A young male Extra comes towards Vivian.

>   EXTRA
> Hallo – lousy morning's work, wasn't it?

                              VIVIAN
     Yes –

                              EXTRA
     Thought I saw you talking to somebody . . .

                              VIVIAN
     I was learning my lines –

                              EXTRA
     Didn't know you had any . . .

He glances at his watch.

     Want a drink? Dutch?

                              VIVIAN
     Later . . . perhaps.

                              EXTRA
     Be seeing you –

He wanders off.

                              VIVIAN
     Mark . . .

                              MARK
     Yes?

                              VIVIAN
                    (*switching off music again*)
     You didn't mind me asking?

                              MARK
     No – more cake?

                              VIVIAN
     No . . . you want to direct . . . more badly than anything . . .
     don't you?

Mark is silent, staring at the sky . . .

     Don't you, Mark?

MARK

I want . . . to photograph . . . the impossible . . .

VIVIAN

What is impossible?

MARK

Something . . . that has never been photographed before –

VIVIAN

What?

MARK

You really want to know . . . ?

VIVIAN

Very much, especially if there's a part for me –

MARK

I want . . . to photograph a murder . . . while it's being committed –

VIVIAN

No part for me then –

MARK

But that . . . isn't enough –

VIVIAN

Is this a new script?

MARK

I want . . . to frighten . . . someone . . . to death . . . and photograph . . . their expression of fear . . .

VIVIAN

Mark! What's this story called?

MARK

That is something . . . *he* never photographed –

VIVIAN

Who?

Mark is silent.

Who *is* he, Mark?

MARK

Anyone –

VIVIAN

No one could . . . they'd be caught –

MARK

I wouldn't care . . . if I had my picture –

VIVIAN

Besides, how would you frighten anyone to death?

MARK

There's a way –

VIVIAN

Well, what?

MARK

There's a way.

VIVIAN

You'd better not tell me! I'll be scared to death tonight as it is!

A hooter.

Back on the set – shall I go first?

MARK

Please –

She rises to her feet . . .

From behind the wall comes a gentle whirring purring sound . . .

VIVIAN

What are you doing?

MARK

Getting into practice –

She smiles down at him.

VIVIAN
See you tonight!

MARK
See you tonight!

She walks away . . .

And the gentle purring continues . . .

Camera pans to the sun beating down on the lot . . .

DISSOLVE TO:

An arc lamp beating down on the set . . .

INT. STUDIO. DAY

Baden bears down on the Assistant Director.

BADEN
Would you enquire if our leading lady is ready to start leading us . . . ?

A cry goes up.

ASSISTANT
(*off*)
Miss Diane Ashley, please! . . . Miss Diane Ashley, please . . .

CLOSE SHOT *of Baden turning towards the entrance.*

CLOSE SHOT *of Mark turning towards the entrance.*

CLOSE SHOT *of entrance.*

INT. STUDIO. DAY

Miss Diane Ashley appears . . . among the many qualities she radiates is goodwill – especially towards Miss Diane Ashley.

DIANE
How are you, Sparks? Chippy? Bob?

VOICES
Hallo, Diane . . .

How are you, Tom? Roger?

Hallo, Diane . . .

And so on, until:

DIANE

How are you, Phil? . . . Mark?

CLOSE SHOT *of Mark.*

MARK

Hallo, Miss Ashley.

DIANE
(*to a figure high in the scaffolding*)
How are you, Pete . . . ?

VOICE

Hi, Di!

She reaches Baden – and completely ignores him.

BADEN

Darling, you've only been playing this part for three weeks, so in case you haven't yet had a chance to read the script –

She ignores this.

– may I remind you that you're a girl with an irresistible impulse!

She looks at him – then at her hand – and nods . . .

– a kleptomaniac! Who cannot help stealing . . . Get inside her, Diane! . . . What – in all the world – do you most want to steal?

DIANE

The limelight!

Baden sighs.

BADEN

We'll run the scene where you catch sight of the store detective and faint . . . Where's the girl who plays the bystander?

Vivian steps forward.

DIANE

How are you?

VIVIAN

Hallo, Diane . . .

1ST ASSISTANT

Positions, everyone!

CLOSE SHOT *of Vivian taking her position in front of the lift. She glances at her watch.*

CLOSE SHOT *of Mark standing by the side of the studio camera. He glances at his watch.*

Camera tracks towards the lift . . .

From Mark's POV we see Diane catch sight of the Store Detective – and crumple in a faint . . .

BADEN

Hit that floor with a thud!

CLOSE SHOT *of door marked:* DON JARVIS – MANAGING DIRECTOR.

(off-screen)

D.J. insists on realism!

A timid knock is overlaid before we dare enter.

INT. EXECUTIVE OFFICE. AFTERNOON

CLOSE SHOT *of a pile of scripts on a great man's desk.*

Camera pulls back –

Mr Jarvis is immersed in reading a script . . . his eyes race across the page.

Over his shoulder we see what he is reading . . . a sheet of figures attached to the script.

*At the same time Mr Jarvis is holding a telephone receiver to his ear –
and we hear an enthusiastic voice filtered through it:*

> VOICE
> (*off-screen*)

– it's a wonderful subject, D.J. . . . Paramount wants it,
M.G.M. wants it, Columbia wants it –

> JARVIS

But is it commercial?

> VOICE
> (*off-screen*)

Danny Angel wants it!

*Still reading the script, Mr Jarvis lays the receiver on his desk and picks
up another.*

> JARVIS

Are those budgets ready? Well bring 'em in –

He replaces this receiver and picks up the original . . .

*The voice is still talking – something about 'a wonderful part for Kenny
or Alec' . . .*

Send me a memo – we'll discuss it next week.

He replaces the receiver.

Miss Simpson enters. She hands him some folders . . . her smile curtsies.

CLOSE SHOT *of Mr Jarvis opening a folder.*

*Over his shoulder we see a page covered with row upon row of
figures . . .*

*The great man's finger skims along the figures like a tailor feeling
cloth . . .*

There's an error! The total should be a hundred and fifty
thousand pounds fourteen shillings and sixpence – not
thirteen and ninepence . . . That could mean the difference
between profit and loss on a first feature!

MISS SIMPSON

Sorry, D.J.

He glowers at her – but his day is made.

JARVIS

Any units working late tonight?

MISS SIMPSON

Only one, sir. Night exteriors on the lot. *The Elephant with Two –*

JARVIS

That animal needs a stick of dynamite!

CLOSE SHOT *of Jarvis.*

Remind me to pay them a visit tonight –

MISS SIMPSON

Yes, D.J.

She makes a note in her little book.

JARVIS

Now, Miss Simpson . . . take a memo to all department heads . . .

Over his shoulder we see an open window . . .

Camera tracks towards it . . .

(*off-screen*)

In light of the new economy drive –

DISSOLVE TO:

CLOSE SHOT *of Clapper Boy's board. It reads: Take 49. The camera pulls back.*

INT. STUDIO. LATE AFTERNOON

BADEN

Again, please . . . and, darling –

He turns to Diane, who is wearily picking herself up off the floor.

– just this once . . . will you *please* make an effort to forget that you're stunning, and *try* to look as if you're stunned . . . ?

> DIANE
> Say one kind word – and I would be!

> ASSISTANT
> (*hastily*)
> Positions, everyone!

DISSOLVE TO:

MONTAGE SEQUENCE:

Camera crew on a tracking shot . . . Mark is operating the Selsen motor.

Baden – shaking his head.

Diane – picking herself up off the floor.

Clapper Boy's board – reading: Take 57.

Vivian – glancing at her watch.

Mark – glancing at his.

Diane – picking herself up off the floor.

> DIANE
> If I have to faint once more I shall faint!

DISSOLVE TO:

CLOSE SHOT *of Baden – triumphant at last.*

> BADEN
> *Cut!* How was that? . . .
> > (*thumbs up all round – with one exception*)
> Mark?

Mark nods perfunctorily.

> Print it!

He glances at his watch – then nods to the Assistant Director.

ASSISTANT

That's it, boys and girls . . . wrap it up! Night-night everyone!

Baden puts his arm round Diane's shoulder.

BADEN

How are you, darling?

She makes a hobbling exit.

CLOSE SHOT *of Vivian hurrying towards the exit carrying her little recorder.*

In a burst of chatter, the unit starts to disperse.

CLOSE SHOT *of Mark picking up his cine-camera and his lunch bag.*

The Clapper Boy comes up to him.

CLAPPER BOY

Catching the bus?

MARK

Not tonight . . . meeting someone . . . for a drink –

CLAPPER BOY

Wanted to discuss the film at the Everyman . . . Tomorrow then?

MARK

I hope so.

CLAPPER BOY

Good night, Mark –

MARK

Good night –

DISSOLVE TO:

CLOSE SHOT *of Vivian. She is sitting at a dressing-room table . . . making-up with care.*

INT. DRESSING ROOM. LATE AFTERNOON

Three other girls share the dressing room with her.

67

There is a knock at the door – and the Young Extra who spoke to Vivian in the grounds pokes his head round.

> EXTRA
>
> Greetings . . . lousy afternoon's work, wasn't it? Who wants a lift to town?

> 1ST GIRL
>
> In what?

> EXTRA
>
> A colleague's car . . . there's room for two on my lap – three at a pinch –

> 1ST GIRL
>
> Which is what we'd get –

> 2ND GIRL
>
> You, Viv?

> VIVIAN
>
> No, thanks . . . I've a date . . . at the Local.

> 1ST GIRL
>
> Us two then?

> 2ND GIRL
>
> I'm game . . . might as well get pinched in a car as squeezed in a tube –

EXT. THE CAR PARK. LATE AFTERNOON

The cars are streaming towards the gate.

CLOSE SHOT *of Baden driving a small new car.*

CLOSE SHOT *of the Chief Cameraman driving a large old one.*

INT. DON JARVIS' OFFICE. LATE AFTERNOON

He is still immersed in his figures.

Miss Simpson is walking to the door. She glances at her little book.

> MISS SIMPSON
>
> I'm to remind you to pay a surprise visit tonight to *The Elephant with* –

68

He grunts.

Good night, D.J. –

Jarvis goes on reading . . .

DISSOLVE TO:

CLOSE SHOT *of Vivian.*

INT. DRESSING ROOM

Music playing. Vivian moves about nervously in front of a mirror in the deserted dressing room. She wears slacks and a shirt. She glances at her watch – her hands are trembling – looks at watch, hears the fireman coming, then switches off the music and hides in the big cupboard –

INT. CORRIDOR

Fireman making his rounds, turning off lights.

EXT. THE CAR PARK. EARLY EVENING

Only a few cars now remain . . . It is beginning to grow dark.

INT. STUDIO CORRIDORS. EARLY EVENING

The long corridors are dim and deserted.

INT. PASSAGE. EARLY EVENING

The fireman is making his rounds.

INT. DRESSING ROOM. EARLY EVENING

Vivian is standing in the cupboard – the lights are on.

INT. CORRIDOR. EARLY EVENING

Fireman opening the dressing-room doors – and glancing inside.

INT. POWER HOUSE. EARLY EVENING

Two electricians are smoking.

INT. CORRIDOR. EARLY EVENING

Fireman opens the door of Vivian's dressing room . . .

INT. DRESSING ROOM. EARLY EVENING

From Vivian's POV we see the lights go out.

We hear the sound of the door closing – and the Fireman's footsteps disappearing down the corridor.

INT. DON JARVIS' OFFICE. EARLY EVENING

The great man closing up his folder . . . glancing at his watch . . . turning out the light . . .

DISSOLVE TO:

INT. CORRIDOR. EARLY EVENING

Vivian is hurrying along a deserted corridor . . . She carries her case and the little recorder.

She pauses – and glances out of a door.

Over her shoulder we see the studio lot – in a blaze of light we can see a crowd of people hanging about in solar topees and tropical kit.

Reverse shot of Vivian watching anxiously.

She turns away – and hurries down the corridor.

EXT. THE COURTYARD. EARLY EVENING

Don Jarvis strides across the courtyard. We can almost hear – and perhaps we do – a cash register ringing up . . .

One of the white-clad figures lounging indolently in the doorway glances round, sees the Inquisition approaching and freezes . . . His degree of terror might satisfy Mark . . .

The great man strides on.

    DISSOLVE TO:

INT. ENTRANCE TO STAGE E. EARLY EVENING

Vivian pauses in front of the entrance to the set.

Above the note is a notice: 'NO ADMITTANCE WHILE RED LIGHT IS ON'.

The light is out . . .

Vivian looks round – there is no one in sight.

Vivian slips in quietly, and closes the door behind her.

INT. STUDIO. EARLY EVENING

The set is in darkness . . .

CLOSE SHOT *of Vivian looking round.*

VIVIAN
(*in a whisper*)

    Mark . . . ?

No reply.

Vivian hesitates . . . then edges slowly forward.

Ahead of her are shadowy counters full of merchandise . . . Beyond them is the door of the lift.

CLOSE SHOT *of the studio camera and the Director's empty chair beside it.*

CLOSE SHOT *of Vivian edging forward.*

Mark –?

She reaches one of the counters – and leans against it, looking around.

Reverse angle shot of Vivian. She is leaning against the counter of the trunk department. Trunks and suitcases at 'greatly reduced prices' are piled behind her.

CLOSE SHOT *of Vivian. She starts whistling nervously under her breath . . .*

Very faintly overlaid is the sound of Mark whistling under his . . .

Vivian stops whistling – and so does Mark . . .

She listens intently for a moment – then peers at her watch . . .

CLOSE SHOT *of the watch on Mark's wrist . . .*

CLOSE SHOT *of Vivian. She shivers suddenly . . . then looks at her watch again . . . She hesitates . . . then turns towards the exit, and starts to edge back . . . She trips over a cable and almost falls . . .*

Suddenly she is bathed in light . . .

She wheels round . . . One of the big spots is beating down on her.

Mark –?

No sign of him. Overlaid is a gentle purring sound . . .

Where are y–

Another light comes on, shining through her hair . . .

Mark!

The sound of his steps is overlaid.

Listen . . . we must –

His footsteps stop . . . she looks round.

Where are you?

His voice is quietly overlaid.

MARK
(*off-screen*)

Here, Viv . . .

She wheels round.

CLOSE SHOT *of Mark sitting in the Director's chair . . . He is holding in his lap his cine-camera, and a black bag.*

CLOSE SHOT *of Vivian breathing quickly.*

VIVIAN

You frightened me!

He looks at her in silence.

Now listen . . . they're working late on the lot –

MARK

I know. They're branched off this stage – I'm using their juice.

He nods, staring at her intently.

VIVIAN

We must call it off . . . someone's bound to see us –

MARK

They might –
(*rising slowly*)
– but they won't interrupt us while we're filming . . . I've put the red light on –

INT. ENTRANCE TO SET. EARLY EVENING

CLOSE SHOT *of the red light – burning.*

CLOSE SHOT *of Vivian.*

INT. STUDIO. EARLY EVENING

VIVIAN

You've what? . . .

MARK

Put the –

VIVIAN

Then they'll know someone's here –

MARK

They won't come in –

VIVIAN

They'll wait outside . . . what's the difference?

MARK

The difference is . . . a perfect film . . .

Over his shoulder we see the studio camera.

I have waited . . . a long time . . . for this . . . and so have you
. . . no one . . . must interrupt it –

She glances round at the brazenly burning lights; shakes her head despairingly.

VIVIAN

We'll be caught –

MARK

What does that matter?

VIVIAN

Matter!

MARK

You stand to lose . . . a job as an extra . . . I stand to lose . . .
nothing –

She looks at him in silence.

. . . the results must be so perfect . . . that the risks don't
count . . .

CLOSE SHOT *of Mark.*

So perfect . . . that even he . . .
                (*he hesitates*)
. . . even he . . . would say . . .

Who? Don Jarvis!?

He looks at her, then nods.

Oh! He'd say:
                (*imitating the great man's voice*)
Sign on the dotted line, kiddies! You can use my pen, but
bring your own ink –
                (*her excitement is growing*)
Mark . . . if you're *sure* it's worth it?

MARK
It's time to find out, Viv . . .

He walks slowly towards the studio camera.

*She prepares for the test by switching on music and warming up with
dance movements.*

VIVIAN
Come on! Get hot!
                (*she accents the rhythm*)

*Mark puts the cine-camera and the black cloth bag on the dolly, slowly
mounts the platform, closes the blimp – and swings the camera.*

*We watch him from the top of the studio, from the door of the studio,
from the Director's chair . . . And finally we watch him from Vivian's
POV. She stops dancing but the music continues.*

You belong there . . .

*He stares ahead of him, his mind far, far away . . . then bends and
looks into the finder.*

*There is a single harsh chord of music – and the screen goes dark. It
remains dark for a moment . . .*

*Suddenly the darkness parts like curtains – and in the centre we see
Vivian's face in the finder of the studio camera. (Unlike the ground-*

glass of the newsagent's camera, we see everything the right way up and in perfect perspective.)

Mark hooks a filler-light below the camera and switches it on. He adjusts the finder until he has made of Vivian's delicate features a radiant miniature.

The miniature smiles shyly at him. She has stopped dancing and is looking directly at the camera. Music continues.

I do feel alone in front of it . . .
> *(she hesitates)*

I suppose stars never do?

MARK
They feel alone without it . . .
> *(he looks in the eyepiece)*

Through the film, we can see only her eyes – large and wistful.

. . . and the great ones . . . feel alone . . . all the time . . .

She becomes the uninhibited Vivian again.

VIVIAN
Then I'm great, boy! What is it you want me to act?
> *(she strikes an attitude à la Robbins)*

He looks up from the camera; she smiles and starts keeping time to the rhythm again.

Being frightened to death?

MARK
You remembered?

VIVIAN
Yes – and I'll have a go!

We hear his quick breathing.

I've been wondering all the afternoon how you'd do it! I'll bet you've thought of a wonderful twist!
> *(she does a wonderful twist)*

CLOSE SHOT *of Mark. He looks down – a little sadly – and peers into the finder. (The camera dolly is on tracks – he tracks forward.)*

Music continues – piano.

In the finder we see a large trunk – 'at greatly reduced prices' – on the shelf behind Vivian.

From Vivian's POV we see Mark leave the studio camera – and hurry towards the trunks . . . She watches him wide-eyed.

What are you doing?

MARK

Building us a set –

He reaches for the largest trunk.

VIVIAN

Why not pull the studio down while you're about it? They can only hang you once –

MARK

Exactly –

He carries the trunk towards the studio camera, and lays it carefully on the floor.

Music continues.

Vivian peers into the front-glass of the studio camera – as if it were a mirror. The rhythm of the music changes.

VIVIAN

If only Don Jarvis could see me now! –

She jumps onto the trunk and taps.

If only I could see Don Jarvis now!

She giggles again.

I warn you, Mark – I'm hysterical . . . I'd rather act dying of laughter, if it's all the same to you . . .

She jumps off the trunk onto the floor.

He opens the trunk . . . she jumps into it.

Her laughter echoes round the deserted studio . . .

DISSOLVE TO:

INT. POWER HOUSE. EARLY EVENING

The two electricians are roaring with laughter. One of them is making tea.

IST ELECTRICIAN
So he did it again! Now *you* tell one –

Camera pans to a dial on the wall . . . one of the needles flickers slightly.

2ND ELECTRICIAN
Half a mo –

He glances at a nearby dial – only a few feet away from the one which is flickering.

> **IST ELECTRICIAN**
> *(off-screen)*

One lump or two?

> **2ND ELECTRICIAN**

As the starlet said to the casting director . . .

He turns away from the dials, and grasps at the outstretched mug.

DISSOLVE TO:

CLOSE SHOT *of Vivian recording – her little recorder is twittering back at great speed.*

> **VIVIAN**
> *(to Mark, over her shoulder)*

What are you doing?

She restarts music.

INT. STUDIO. EARLY EVENING

She is watching Mark curiously as he arranges the lighting.

> **MARK**

Be patient, Viv . . . it's going to be worth it –

CLOSE SHOT *of the studio camera. In front of it – fixed on a small hook – is a tape measure . . .*

Mark reaches for it . . . then carefully measures the distance between the trunk and the camera . . . then he takes a piece of chalk from his pocket and makes a small cross on the floor.

The music continues.

> **VIVIAN**

Oh well! I've stood alone in front of a studio camera! That's more than most have –

> **MARK**

Ever stood . . . behind one?

> **VIVIAN**

No –

MARK

Help yourself.

She goes around the camera out of sight – and he is out of hers.

He glances into the trunk – it is deep, and very empty.

VIVIAN
(*accenting the rhythm*)
I can see you, Mark – perfectly!

MARK

Good . . .

VIVIAN

Yes, sir! I'll bet I'm the best camerawoman in the business! . . .
(*beating time with her feet*)

Mark hurries to the side of the studio camera and picks up his cine-camera.

(*off-screen*)
I've lost you!

MARK

I'll be back –

Suddenly Mark's face appears in the finder.

VIVIAN

Welcome, stranger!

We see Mark raise his cine-camera. He seems to be pointing it straight at us.

We hear a gentle purring.

What are you doing?

MARK
Photographing you photographing me . . .

High angle shot of Mark standing in front of the studio camera – photographing her photographing him . . .

VIVIAN
(*in mock awe*)
Mark, you're brilliant . . .

He walks slowly towards her, holding his cine-camera to his eyes.

In the finder of Mark's cine-camera we see Vivian at the studio camera . . . She comes closer and closer . . .

(*off-screen*)
Lost you again!

MARK
Never mind –

We see him standing almost on top of her – his cine-camera trained on her.

I'm ready now, Viv . . .

She looks up slowly – and a little hesitantly.

Music, all drums.

Go and stand on that cross, will you?

VIVIAN
(*solemnly*)
Yes, sir, Mr Director, sir –

He watches her in silence as she walks to the front of the studio camera and takes up her position . . . while the drum-beat continues.

DISSOLVE TO:

EXT. COURTYARD. EARLY EVENING

Don Jarvis is leaving the unit working on the lot. It is now bustling with activity.

A girl comes up to him . . . She raises her cigarette for a light – and looks into his eyes.

He hands her a box of matches . . . and walks away.

Over his shoulder we see the other stages – apparently empty. Don Jarvis hesitates, then strides towards one.

81

INT. POWER HOUSE. EARLY EVENING

CLOSE SHOT *of a dial – the needle flickering slightly.*

Overlaid is the voice of the 1st Electrician.

> 1ST ELECTRICIAN
> (*off-screen*)
> – and here's one of the wife and nipper –

DISSOLVE TO:

INT. STUDIO. EARLY EVENING

CLOSE SHOT *of Vivian staring at the trunk on the floor behind her. The recorded rhythm continues.*

> VIVIAN
> Am I supposed to imagine someone is going to put me in there?

Mark is watching her over the top of the studio camera.

> MARK
> Yes, Viv . . .

He peers into the viewfinder.

In the finder we see Vivian looking rather pathetically into camera.

> VIVIAN
> Mark – I hope I won't let you down . . . I know you're trying to create atmosphere for me – but . . . I just don't feel frightened! Wouldn't it be better if I just did my number?

> MARK
> (*shaking head*)
> Later.

> VIVIAN
> Oh all right! I could do anything – I feel so relaxed – and that's due to you . . . You're so at home with that camera you make *me* feel at home too . . . you have it in you, boy!

From her POV we see him raise his head slightly.

MARK

Ready, Viv?

VIVIAN
(*great effort*)

Well – I'll try –

In the finder we see her wrinkling her brow . . .

But what . . . would . . . frighten me to death –?
(*looking appealingly into camera*)
Set the mood for me, Mark . . .

MARK

Well . . .

He goes and switches off the recorder. The sudden silence is startling.

Imagine someone . . . coming towards you . . . who's going
to kill you – regardless of consequences . . .

VIVIAN

A madman?

MARK

Yes – but he knows it . . . and you don't . . . and just to kill
you . . . isn't enough for him –

VIVIAN

But how would he frighten me to –?

*She stares into focusing screen – intrigued, but not frightened, not even
by the silence and shadowy vastness around her.*

MARK

Stay there, Viv . . . you're . . . just right –

She stands motionless – staring into camera.

INT. CORRIDOR IN STUDIO. EARLY EVENING

CLOSE SHOT *of Don Jarvis. He is standing motionless, staring down a
corridor.*

*What he is staring at is out of camera – and it is puzzling the great
man.*

He walks quietly along the corridor.

CLOSE SHOT *of Vivian.*

> VIVIAN
> I can't imagine what you've thought of!

INT. STUDIO. EARLY EVENING

CLOSE SHOT *of Mark. He raises his head slowly – and locks the studio camera off. Then he walks slowly towards her . . .*

HIGH ANGLE SHOT *of Mark walking towards Vivian.*

Camera zooms down to the trunk behind her.

Mark's voice is overlaid:

> MARK
> (*off-screen*)
> Suppose this . . . were one of his weapons . . .

CLOSE SHOT *of Don Jarvis.*

INT. CORRIDOR. EARLY EVENING

The great man is poised for the kill. He is moving forward stealthily . . . and suddenly breaks into a run . . .

Camera pans – and we see the object of his attentions . . .

A wisp of smoke is coming from behind an alcove . . .

CLOSE SHOT *of a Fireman – smoking a cigarette.*

CLOSE SHOT *of Don Jarvis – smoking!*

CLOSE SHOT *of the Fireman's terror as he sees Don Jarvis.*

> JARVIS
> Smoking on duty!

The Fireman opens his mouth to explain – and smoke exudes.

> Come with me!

The Fireman follows him meekly.

Camera pans . . .

So near – yet a lifetime away – a red light is burning above a closed door.

CLOSE SHOT *of Vivian – puzzled.*

> VIVIAN
>
> That –?

INT. STUDIO. EARLY EVENING

CLOSE SHOT *of Mark.*

He is holding his cine-camera; fixed to it is a collapsible tripod.

Suddenly he pulls one leg of the tripod out . . . We see that a very sharp spike protrudes from the end of it.

From Mark's POV we see Vivian looking at the spike.

He raises it towards her – until the spike is only inches from her throat . . .

> Yes . . . that would be frightening –

> MARK
>
> But . . . there's something else . . .

We can hear his heart pounding as if it will burst – and gradually Vivian, too, becomes aware of it.

> VIVIAN
>
> Well? What is it?

Just for a moment Mark's arm moves. His back hides what he is doing . . .

Suddenly we see Vivian turn her head sharply – she is looking at something out of camera.

> (in a whisper)
>
> That . . . ?

The spike is very close to her throat – but Vivian ignores it, staring out of camera.

Over Mark's shoulder we concentrate on Vivian's face . . .
(in a whisper)

     Mark . . . take it –

The fear on her face is rapidly growing . . .

    – away –

She tries to move back – but the trunk prevents her.

    MARK – YOU –

It is almost a scream . . .

We can hear Mark breathing quickly.

Vivian raises her hands to push something away from her . . .

Suddenly the screen is filled with her eyes . . . We see them dilating with terror. There is a sudden crash as the big power switches go out in the roof.

The lights go out.

There is a scream in the darkness.

Then silence.

The darkness acquires a grey, opaque quality as if one is seeing the world through a curtain – it is the world of Mrs Stephens.

A bright light is felt, rather than seen, beating against our eyelids. It looms closer and stronger.

> HELEN'S VOICE
>
> And that, darling, is the end of the news! Unless you want the football results?

CLOSE SHOT *of Mrs Stephens, a large glass of whisky – and the bottle – beside her. It is night.*

> MRS STEPHENS
>
> No thank you.

CLOSE SHOT *of Helen. 'She's Got the Key of the Door' is overlaid.*

> HELEN
>
> What else can I read you?

> MRS STEPHENS
>
> The label on this whisky bottle! Are you *sure* it says seventy per cent proof?

> HELEN
>
> Certain.

> MRS STEPHENS
>
> They're bigger liars than the press –

From Helen's POV we see her reach for her glass with a steady hand.

> HELEN
>
> Is that your last tonight?

> MRS STEPHENS
>
> I doubt it.

> HELEN
>
> Your last but one?

> MRS STEPHENS
>
> Don't haggle –

HELEN
(*producing a coin*)
Toss me double or nothing?

MRS STEPHENS
Done!

Helen spins the coin on the table . . . Mrs Stephens listens intently . . .
the coin stops spinning.

Heads –

Her fingers shoot out and feel the surface of the coin.

HELEN
Bad luck, darling –

MRS STEPHENS
Huh –

She turns the coin over and carefully feels the other side. Helen watches
her with a smile – then looks thoughtfully at the ceiling.

What are you looking at?

HELEN
The ceiling!

MRS STEPHENS
Wondering if that young man is home?

HELEN
Yes.

MRS STEPHENS
Well he is . . . I heard him come in . . . four paragraphs ago –

From Helen's POV we see the sightless eyes staring at her.

Do you like him?

CLOSE SHOT *of Helen.*

HELEN
Yes, darling –

                              MRS STEPHENS
Why?

                                 HELEN
He has a quality . . .

                              MRS STEPHENS
                            (*sipping her glass*)
Wish this had –

                                 HELEN
. . . and I think he could help me –

                              MRS STEPHENS
With your photographs?

                                 HELEN
Yes . . .

CLOSE SHOT *of Mrs Stephens.*

                              MRS STEPHENS
Helen . . .

                                 HELEN
Yes?

Mrs Stephens hesitates – which is rare.

                              MRS STEPHENS
                               (*abruptly*)
It doesn't matter –

                                 HELEN
                               (*quickly*)
Mummy, what's worrying you?

                              MRS STEPHENS
The price of whisky.

                                 HELEN
What else?

                              MRS STEPHENS
What else matters?

HELEN

Don't you like Mark?

MRS STEPHENS

Haven't met him –

HELEN

You don't like him! Now why not?

CLOSE SHOT *of Mrs Stephens. Again she hesitates.*

MRS STEPHENS

I distrust a man who walks quietly –

HELEN

He's shy!

MRS STEPHENS

His footsteps aren't! They're stealthy . . .

HELEN

Now darling –

MRS STEPHENS

Are you going up to him?

HELEN

May I?

MRS STEPHENS

We both have the key of the door . . . Mine needs oiling –
and yours needs exercise . . . Off you go –

HELEN

Thank you –

She kisses her – and glances at the whisky glass.

– remember that you lost the toss.

She walks to the door.

MRS STEPHENS

Helen . . .

HELEN

Yes, darling?

MRS STEPHENS

If you're back in five minutes . . . I won't even finish this –

HELEN

Done!

She hurries out . . . Mrs Stephens instantly refills her glass.

CLOSE SHOT *of her hand . . . It has begun to tremble.*

MARK'S DARK-ROOM

CLOSE SHOT *of Mark's hands, in the green light of the dark-room. He is busy unloading and winding film onto a developing rack.*

He puts the rack of exposed film into the tank and starts the time clock.

CLOSE SHOT *of the time clock ticking.*

A knock is heard off.

Mark looks up.

MARK

Who is it?

HELEN
(*off-screen*)

Helen . . .

CLOSE SHOT *of Mark.*

Faintly overlaid is 'She's Got the Key of the Door'.

He looks down at the clock.

MARK
(*calling*)

Come in – Helen –

INT. PASSAGE. EVENING

Helen opens the door of Mark's sitting room. We hear Mark call out from the inner room:

MARK
(*off-screen*)
Would you . . . please . . . wait in there? . . . Developing –

Helen goes in, closing the door behind her.

INT. MARK'S SITTING ROOM. EVENING

Helen enters. She speaks loudly to be heard in the dark-room.

HELEN
Mother heard you come in – so I guessed you wouldn't be in bed . . .

No reply from the inner room.

Are you sure this is conven–

MARK
(*off-screen*)
Won't be long –

Helen glances at her watch . . . then looks curiously round the room.

CLOSE SHOT *of Vivian's recorder, placed on a chair.*

CLOSE SHOT *of Helen. She picks it up and looks at it, curiously, fingering the stops . . .*

MARK
(*off-screen*)
Hallo.

Helen turns round. Mark is standing on the threshold of the dark-room.

HELEN
Hallo, Mark . . .

He walks towards her . . . he stops suddenly. He is staring at the recorder in her hand.

I hope you don't mind – is it a tape-recorder?

MARK
Yes –

93

Gently he takes it from her – as if it is a cup with which she has finished – and replaces it on the shelf.

CLOSE SHOT *of Helen.*

> HELEN
>
> I'm sure I'm being a nuisance . . . but, Mark, I very much want to . . .

Her voice trails away.

CLOSE SHOT *of Mark. He is holding out a small package.*

> MARK
>
> Happy birthday.

> HELEN
>
> Mark! That's very sweet of you – but really –

> MARK
>
> It isn't much . . . I don't know anything about . . . presents for twenty-one . . . but I saw it this morning . . . so . . . please –

> HELEN
> (*gently*)
>
> Thank you . . .

She takes the package, and unwraps it. Inside is a slender brooch . . . it is not expensive but it is made with great care.

> It's beautiful . . .

> MARK
>
> I like the design . . . More milk?

> HELEN
>
> More? . . . No, thank you, Mark . . . and I really appreciate this . . . I'm going to put it on now.

He watches her hold it against her dress.

> There? . . . Or there? . . .

> MARK
>
> The first place . . .

I think so too! . . .

CLOSE SHOT *of Helen pinning it on.*

CLOSE SHOT *of Mark touching his lapel.*

CLOSE SHOT *of Helen glancing at her watch.*

CLOSE SHOT *of Mark glancing at his . . . He thinks of the ticking clock
in the dark-room.*

Helen looks up, and sees him.

I *am* keeping you.

MARK

No . . . I promise –

HELEN

Mark, I'm here for some advice –

MARK

From me?

HELEN

Please . . .

*He looks as if he has just been voted the best cameraman of the year
(unanimously) – and the two films he directed have both won Oscars
(though Don Jarvis understood them).*

His delighted astonishment is such that she has to smile.

. . . I work in a public library – in the children's section . . .
I'm telling you that to postpone admitting what always
embarrasses me . . .

She takes a deep breath.

In my spare time . . . I write –

MARK

What's embar–

HELEN

I write stories for children . . . but so did Grimm . . . Hans
Andersen . . . Lewis Carroll . . .

MARK

Had any published?

HELEN

Some short stories –

MARK

I'd like to read –

HELEN

I learned today . . . that my first book . . . has been accepted!
. . . For publication in the spring . . .

MARK

But that's wonderful . . . what's it about?

HELEN

A magic camera – and what it photographs . . .

CLOSE SHOT *of Mark.*

MARK

Whatever made you . . . think of that?

HELEN

I'll tell you one day – I promise . . .

MARK

Well *what* does it photograph?

HELEN

I'll tell you that too – but, Mark . . . this is the problem . . .
The children who read the book will want to *see* the pictures
the camera takes – but the publishers say they're impossible to
photograph, and suggest drawings . . . but I don't agree –

MARK

No – nothing's impossible –

I was hoping you'd say that! There *must* be photographs –
however difficult to take – and I was wondering, Mark – if
you'd –

MARK

Oh yes –

HELEN

– discuss it with me –

MARK

– take them –

HELEN

Mark – I can't ask you to do that . . .

They have cancelled his Oscar.

I mean . . . the publisher's mightn't agree –

MARK

I'd take them . . . for you –

HELEN

Yes but . . . the money –

MARK

There are some things . . . which I photograph . . . for
nothing –

HELEN

I didn't mean to offend you –

MARK

Offend?

CLOSE SHOT *of Mark.*

Helen . . . if you knew what it meant . . . for something to
happen to me . . . that I don't have to *make* happen . . . it's
like . . . you've given me a twenty-first birthday . . .

CLOSE SHOT *of Helen looking at him . . .*

What does your camera photograph?

HELEN

Mark – I *must* go . . . I just wanted to know . . . if you'd talk it over with me –

MARK

When please?

HELEN

That's up to you –

MARK

Helen . . . I don't know much about . . . dinner out . . . but would you come with me?

HELEN

Thank you –

MARK

Thank you –

HELEN

When?

MARK

Oh . . .

HELEN

What's the matter?

MARK

It had better be soon . . .

HELEN

Are you going away?

MARK

Almost for certain! . . .

HELEN

Oh . . . well you suggest when –

MARK

Are you free . . . tomorrow night?

HELEN

Yes –

MARK

I hope I am!

HELEN

I'll understand if you're not –

MARK

I'll try to be – I'll try my hardest to be.

HELEN

Thank you for listening . . . and for my present.

MARK

– and for mine.

They look at each other in silence.

HELEN

Good night, Mark . . .
                    (*turning to the door*)

MARK

Good night . . . Helen . . .

He watches her leave, standing very still . . .

Off stage, the time clock explodes.

CLOSE SHOT – *the excited clock. Mark's hand silences it.*

INT. DARK-ROOM. GREEN LIGHT

Mark opens the developing tank, lifts out the rack of film, drops it into the fixing bath.

He switches light from green to red.

CLOSE SHOT – *green to red dark-room lamp.*

Mark lifts the rack of glistening film out of the fixing bath and scans the image.

CLOSE SHOT – *Mark's face and the tell-tale black and white images.*

CLOSE SHOT – *the film. A pile of trunks.*

In the darkness we hear a man enquire softly:

Looking for a trunk?

CLOSE SHOT *of a Tall Man with a severe face. He is standing in front of a familiar pile of trunks marked at 'Specially Reduced Prices'.*

Camera pulls back slowly – and we see whom he is addressing . . . It is Diane.

Camera pulls further back and we see that we are in a small theatre watching rushes . . .

INT. THEATRE IN STUDIO. DAY

Camera pans across Baden's disgruntled face . . . the Chief Cameraman's bored face . . . the Script Girl's puzzled face . . . to Diane's expression of rapture as she watches herself on the screen.

DIANE
(*off-screen*)
I'd like to see that one –

From Diane's POV we watch the screen. We see the Tall Man (shop assistant) reaching for a trunk and laying it on the counter . . . He opens it with a flourish . . . Vivian passes across the screen – glances casually at the trunk – and wanders off . . .

BADEN
No – no – no – we must get some comedy into this . . . !

The Assistant Director nods.

We'll retake it this morning . . .

Camera lingers for a moment on the screen as Diane (on-screen) smiles at the Assistant –

DIANE
(*she pockets a small item*)
I'll take it –

The Assistant bows and closes the trunk . . . We dissolve to the set itself –

INT. STUDIO. DAY

The Assistant is leaning over the counter, listening intently. Diane stands in front of the counter, receiving the attentions of the Make-up Man.

Baden's voice is overlaid:

> BADEN
> (*off-screen*)
> I want some comedy in this scene . . .

Camera pulls back.

The unit is busy preparing for a retake. The studio camera (and its crew) are off camera, and we concentrate on Baden briefing his artistes.

He is clutching a script as if afraid that opening it might be indecent exposure.

> Instead of taking the first trunk you see, I want you, darling
> . . . to ask for a blue trunk – and when he brings it to you, to
> ask for a red one – and when he brings that, to ask for a white
> one . . .
> (*turns to the Assistant*)
> And you, Michael . . . get the trunks one by one – growing
> more and more fed up – and we'll end on a gag which I'll
> think of in a minute – all right?

> DIANE
> I don't feel it!

> BADEN
> Don't feel it! *Do it!*

> ASSISTANT DIRECTOR
> (*hastily*)
> Positions, everyone!

Over Mark's shoulder – behind the camera – we watch the Unit taking up positions.

> Anyone seen Vivian?

> BADEN
> Who?

> ASSISTANT DIRECTOR
> The red-headed bystander – *Viv* –

> BADEN
> (*impatiently*)
Never mind – I'm cutting her out of this scene . . . Let's run it –

> ASSISTANT DIRECTOR
> (*shouting*)
Quiet, everyone!

From Mark's POV we watch the scene being rehearsed. Diane approaches the trunk counter and the Assistant smiles at her.

> ASSISTANT
Can I interest you in a trunk?

> DIANE
Thank you . . .
> (*pointing*)
I'd like to see that one . . .

> ASSISTANT
Certainly, madam . . .

He turns away . . . She pockets a small item from the counter. He heaves a trunk forward.

It's beautifully fitted –
> (*he opens it*)

She takes a perfunctory glance –

> DIANE
I'd like to see one in red –

> ASSISTANT
Certainly, madam –

She pockets another item.

He turns and wrestles with another trunk . . . brings it forward and opens it . . .

> DIANE
. . . do you have one in white?

ASSISTANT

Certainly, madam.

*Mark walks away quietly from the back of the Camera Crew. He
hurries to the shelf where he keeps his cine-camera and a lunch basket
. . . He reaches for his camera.*

Diane's voice is overlaid.

DIANE
(*off-screen*)

Do you have one in blue?

ASSISTANT
(*off-screen*)

Certainly, madam . . .

*Mark turns towards the rehearsal and raises his cine-camera . . . We
see the Assistant try to lift a blue trunk – and half collapse with the
weight of it . . .*

CLOSE SHOT *of Baden . . . beaming.*

*The Assistant manages to drag the trunk forward. He leans over it –
exhausted – then starts to open it . . .*

Mark moves round until Diane's face is in the finder . . .

*As the lid of the trunk is opened we can see only her eyes above the rim
of the lid . . . We hear her scream –*

CLOSE SHOT *of Baden . . . freezing.*

There is the sound of a body falling to the ground . . .

BADEN

The silly bitch! She's fainted in the wrong scene . . .

FADE OUT:

*In the darkness we hear a telephone ringing . . . and then another . . .
and then another . . . then they all merge into one big blast –*

FADE IN:

Camera tracks quickly towards a door marked PUBLICITY
DEPARTMENT.

INT. PUBLICITY DEPARTMENT. DAY

The Head of publicity has a receiver to his ear.

HEAD OF PUBLICITY

– is this a gag? . . . A girl in a trunk! . . . Who is she? . . .
Well, which unit? . . . *The walls are closing in?* . . . What a
break for them! . . . I mean what a heartbreak –
(*he is already speaking into another telephone*)
– call a press conference.
(*he turns to the original telephone*)
I'm on my way down –

EXT. LONDON. DAY

A police car. There are two men seated at the back.

INT. POLICE CAR. DAY

*Chief Inspector Gregg is reading a file . . . A plain-clothes Sergeant
(Miller) is seated next to him . . . The Sergeant glances at his Chief
apprehensively.*

SERGEANT MILLER

Excuse me, Chief –

CHIEF INSPECTOR

Mm?

SERGEANT MILLER

We pass my house when we reach the bypass. Would you
mind if I drop off for a minute?

CHIEF INSPECTOR
(*without raising his eyes*)
To collect your kid's autograph book?

SERGEANT MILLER

Yes, Chief! . . . If the nipper hears where I've been . . .

CHIEF INSPECTOR
(*turns to the driver*)
All right, Dawson – anything to help the Sergeant –
(*stares down at the folder*)

– and it's about time the Sergeant helped me – we're getting nowhere with this.

Over his shoulder we see what he is looking at – it is a photograph of Dora in her furs and finery.

SERGEANT
What about that man the landlady passed –

CHIEF INSPECTOR
She couldn't describe him – except to say that he was carrying something that she couldn't see –

SERGEANT
That's a help –

CLOSE SHOT *of the Inspector staring at the folder.*

CHIEF INSPECTOR
Sergeant, I've been on the force thirty odd years . . . and I have never seen such fear on anyone's face as on this girl's . . .
              (*almost to himself*)
What was it she saw?

SERGEANT
Surely, Chief . . . a man coming at her – with a sharp weapon –

CHIEF INSPECTOR
I'm familiar with that kind of terror. This is something new to me . . . but *what?*

The Sergeant glances at Dora's photograph.

– now take a look at how we found her –

He starts to turn the page . . .

DISSOLVE TO:

A door with a sign on it: CANTEEN CLOSED TODAY.

Camera tracks towards it . . .

INT. CANTEEN. DAY

Mark is sitting by an open window at the far end of the canteen. His cine-camera and lunch basket are by his side.

From Mark's POV we see that the unit (with the exception of Diane and Baden) is crowded into the canteen.

They have formed themselves into small groups and are talking in whispers.

The Assistant Director is standing with his back to the door. A girl calls out:

> GIRL
> (*off-screen*)
> How much longer must we wait in here?

> ASSISTANT DIRECTOR
> Till the police arrive . . . D.J.'s orders –

Mark glances at a group in the corner.

The Trunk Assistant is encircled by eager listeners.

> ASSISTANT
> – and when she opened that trunk . . . and I saw what was inside . . . my dears – I nearly fainted with her –
> (*he runs a delicate hand across a delicate forehead*)
> – and do you know what horrified me most?

> ASSISTANT DIRECTOR
> D.J. says not to discuss it –

> ASSISTANT
> Any more sauce from D.J. and I shall refuse to sign for seven years! My dears . . . that poor girl's expression –

Mark glances out of the window . . .

From his POV we see a police car driving across the courtyard. Mark watches with great interest – then reaches for his cine-camera.

He photographs the police, then puts his cine-camera on to the table and sits back . . . waiting . . . Camera lingers for a moment on the folded tripod.

INT. SET. DAY

The set is completely deserted. It is lit by a single lamp. A solitary trunk stands on the counter, its lid closed.

We see Don Jarvis enter, followed by the two Policemen. Baden and the Publicity man bring up the rear.

Don Jarvis points towards the trunks department. The Chief Inspector nods, then he and the Sergeant approach the counter.

Carefully the Inspector raises the lid of the trunk – he looks inside.

CLOSE SHOT *of the Inspector – over the top of the lid. His expression is mainly one of surprise.*

CLOSE SHOT *of the Sergeant staring into the trunk. He is also surprised – but there is nausea in his face.*

They look up at almost the same moment . . . their eyes meet.

> SERGEANT
> *(in a whisper)*
>
> Chief, it's exactly the –

> INSPECTOR
>
> I know . . .
> *(he closes the trunk quickly. Quietly)*
> – don't say anything –
> *(he faces Don Jarvis)*
> Well, sir . . . we shall probably have to interview everyone at the studio, so we'd better plan a campaign that won't interfere too much with your productions –

> JARVIS
> *(warming to him at once)*
>
> Thank you, Chief Inspector . . . if you knew what even a single day's delay could cost –

> INSPECTOR
>
> Oh, we do sir –
> *(his eyes are on the trunk)*

DISSOLVE TO:

CLOSE SHOT *of Mark.*

INT. CANTEEN. DAY

He is looking out of the window – his camera at the ready.

Overlaid is the sound of a door opening . . . the buzz of conversation dies away . . .

We hear Don Jarvis' voice . . .

> JARVIS
>
> If I may have your attention, please –

A hand tugs at Mark's elbow. He turns round . . .

The Clapper Boy looks at him warningly . . .

From Mark's POV we see Don Jarvis standing in the doorway – facing a suddenly hushed room. The great man's hands are folded in front of him –

> The police wish to interview each of you individually . . . after which you will be at liberty to leave –

From D.J.'s POV we see the upturned faces – the light from the window falls upon Mark, listening to him with rapt attention . . . Mark's hands are folded in front of him.

> – there will, of course, be no shooting today . . . but work will be resumed, as usual, tomorrow . . . with, I hope, all of you present –

CLOSE SHOT *of Don Jarvis.*

> I look to you to give the police your fullest cooperation.
> (*he turns abruptly and leaves*)

Sergeant Miller enters with a smile.

> SERGEANT MILLER
>
> Well now . . . let's get ourselves organized . . .
> (*taking a piece of paper from his pocket*)
> We don't want to keep you cooped up in here, so we've

worked out a timetable . . . We'll talk to the artists first, then the technicians in this order . . .

Mark reaches for his cine-camera . . .

DISSOLVE TO:

A series of brief shots of the unit being interviewed by the police.

EXT. STUDIO GROUNDS. DAY

The Young Extra who spoke to Vivian in the exterior set points excitedly to the wall where Vivian and Mark lay.

The Inspector and Sergeant carefully examine both sides of the wall . . . The Inspector stoops, picks up something with a pair of tweezers and puts it in an envelope . . .

Camera pans –

A few passers-by look on from a distance . . . One of them is watching through his cine-camera.

DISSOLVE TO:

INT. SMALL OFFICE. DAY

The Young Extra who shared Vivian's dressing room is talking to the Chief Inspector and Sergeant –

> EXTRA
> – she said she didn't want a lift – because she had a call to make locally . . .

> CHIEF INSPECTOR
> Did she say where?

> EXTRA
> No, sir . . . and when I left, she was still in the dressing room –

> CHIEF INSPECTOR
> I see . . . let's have a look at this dressing room, shall we?

EXTRA
Yes, sir . . .

INT. PASSAGE IN STUDIO. DAY

The Policemen and the Extra are walking away from camera down a passage. A few members of other units pass them by without a glance . . .

One of these (a girl) smiles into camera.

GIRL

Hallo, Mark . . .

MARK
(*off-screen*)

Hallo –

The girl walks out of picture.

The camera (and Mark) track after the Policemen.

INT. ENTRANCE TO DRESSING ROOM. DAY

As the Inspector opens the door of the dressing room, Mark hurries past . . . He raises his cine-camera and photographs the Sergeant . . .

The Sergeant turns to close the door . . . He sees Mark . . . straightens his tie and looks as severe as he can.

SERGEANT

Hey, I don't think you ought to do that –

MARK

Sorry, sir –

He hurries down the passage.

INSPECTOR
(*turning round*)

Do what?

SERGEANT

Make me famous. Some chap was giving me a screen test –

The Extra's voice is overlaid – a hint of hysteria in it –

(*off-screen*)
That's where she sat, Inspector –

The Inspector turns away, and the Sergeant closes the door.

DISSOLVE TO:

INT. SMALL OFFICE. DAY

The door of the small office opens – and the Chief Cameraman comes out.

Camera pans –

On a bench at the end of the passage Mark, the Clapper Boy, and a member of the camera-crew are waiting.

VOICE
And whoever did it must be . . .

CHIEF CAMERAMAN
You're next –

The Crew-member hurries into the office, and closes the door . . . The Chief Cameraman wanders off thoughtfully.

Mark and the Clapper Boy are left sitting side by side.

CLAPPER BOY
I've been watching you . . .

MARK
Oh?

CLAPPER BOY
Have you been filming those policemen?

MARK
Yes, I've a few quite interesting shots of them – it's a chance I never expected!

CLAPPER BOY
A chance for what?

III

MARK

To photograph . . . an investigation . . . or as much of it as I can –

CLAPPER BOY

What on earth for?

MARK

It will complete a documentary I'm making –

CLAPPER BOY

– documentary?

Mark nods.

What's it about?

MARK

I'd rather not tell you till it's finished. And it soon will be . . .

CLAPPER BOY

But suppose they catch you –

MARK

Oh they will – they look very efficient.

CLAPPER BOY

Don't you mind?

MARK

No.

CLAPPER BOY

But they might confiscate your camera –

MARK

I'm afraid they will! But by then . . . I'll have finished with it –

CLAPPER BOY

I don't –

The door of the small room opens, and the Crew-member comes out.

CREW-MEMBER

You, Mark –

MARK

Thanks . . .

He rises slowly . . . the cine-camera is over his shoulder.

CLAPPER BOY

Mark, hadn't you better leave that with me?

MARK

No, John –

CLAPPER BOY

I'd look after it –

MARK

I'm sure of that – but I'd like to photograph them while
they're questioning me –

The Clapper Boy looks at him in amazement.

I don't suppose they'll let me –

CLAPPER BOY

Mark, are you potty?

MARK

Yes, do you think they'll notice?

The Clapper Boy laughs.

CLAPPER BOY

Don't get into any trouble for heaven's sake – I want to
discuss that film at the Everyman . . .

MARK

Yes . . . I'd like that . . .

He walks slowly towards the door.

The Clapper Boy takes out a copy of Sight and Sound *and starts to
read it.*

INT. SMALL OFFICE. DAY

*The Inspector is seated at a desk, reading some notes . . . The Sergeant
is seated by the side of the desk, a pile of papers in front of him.*

There is a gentle knock on the door.

The Sergeant glances at a list.

> SERGEANT
>
> Mark Lewis – focus-puller . . . Whatever that may be –

The Inspector nods.

> Come in.

He puts a tick on the list . . . There is the sound of a door opening . . .

The Inspector looks up . . .

From his POV we see a young man with a camera over his shoulder advancing shyly towards him.

> INSPECTOR
>
> Mr Lewis?

> MARK
>
> Yes, sir . . .

> INSPECTOR
>
> I'm Chief Inspector Gregg and this is Sergeant Miller. Grab a chair –

The Sergeant glances up.

> SERGEANT
>
> Ah! My photographer –

> MARK
>
> I've brought the camera in case you want to take the film away –

He holds out his camera.

The Sergeant glances enquiringly at the Inspector.

> INSPECTOR
>
> That's all right, Mr Lewis – as long as we don't appear at the Odeon next week in place of the cartoon –

Mark smiles.

MARK

Thank you, sir.

INSPECTOR

Well now; have you anything to tell us?

MARK

I don't think so, sir.

INSPECTOR

Did you know the girl?

MARK

Yes, sir . . .

INSPECTOR

How well?

MARK

Mainly by sight –

INSPECTOR

When did you see her last?

He picks up a pencil – taps it idly on the desk.

MARK

Yesterday afternoon – when we broke . . .

INSPECTOR

Speak to her?

MARK

Called out good night – don't know if she heard –

CLOSE SHOT *of Mark's fingers . . . tapping on his knee in time to the pencil.*

INSPECTOR

What did you do then?

MARK

Took some shots, sir – for a film I'm making –

INSPECTOR

Oh . . . where?

MARK

All over the place, sir . . . it's a documentary –

INSPECTOR

Anyone with you?

MARK

No, sir. Just my camera –

INSPECTOR

What time did you arrive home, Mr Lewis?

MARK

About ten . . . ten-thirty . . .

INSPECTOR

Anyone see you?

MARK

Yes . . . the people downstairs.

INSPECTOR

I see –

The telephone rings . . .

The Sergeant promptly answers it.

SERGEANT
Sergeant Miller – Right, I'll tell him . . .

He replaces the receiver, turns to the Inspector.

The doctor's finished his examin–

The Inspector rises at once –

– wants to see you –

INSPECTOR
Right –
(he glances at Mark)
That'll be all for the moment, Mr Lewis – thank you –

MARK
Thank you, sir . . .
(he turns to the door)

INSPECTOR
Wait a minute.

Mark stands very still.

– direct me to that set of yours, will you? I'd probably end on location –

MARK
I'll take you there, sir –
(he opens the door)

INSPECTOR
Thanks –
(he glances at the Sergeant)
Carry on with the interviews, Sergeant –

SERGEANT
Yes, sir –

From the Sergeant's POV we see Mark turn to go into the passage . . .

The Sergeant stares at the camera on his shoulder . . . then the door closes . . .

The Sergeant makes a note on a piece of paper.

INT. PASSAGE. DAY

The Inspector and Mark walk side by side along the passage. The Clapper Boy comes into view – still reading Sight and Sound.

The Clapper Boy glances up – just in time to see the Inspector and Mark walk side by side to the end of the corridor . . .

CLAPPER BOY
(*staring after them*)

I warned him to be careful!

DISSOLVE TO:

INT. ENTRANCE TO SET. DAY

A Constable is standing outside the entrance to the set.

From his POV we see the Inspector and Mark approach.

The Constable stiffens . . .

From Mark's POV we see the Constable barring the entrance . . .

INSPECTOR

I think I can find my way now –

Mark smiles . . .

– thanks for the escort –

The Inspector hurries towards the door of the set.

The Constable opens it – and the Inspector goes inside.

The Constable closes the door – and stands in front of it.

Mark turns away quickly.

DISSOLVE TO:

EXT. COURTYARD. DAY

The car park is jammed with cars – but there is hardly anyone in sight. Mark hurries towards the large sliding doors of Stage E – they are a few feet apart. He looks round carefully, then slips inside . . .

INT. STAGE E. DAY

Facing Mark is the darkened set of an hotel bedroom. Beyond this is another set – also in darkness – and beyond this yet another. Only in the far corner of the studio – in the furthermost set – is there a light burning. Voices can faintly be heard coming from this set.

Mark walks quietly towards a long ladder which leads up to the gantry. Carefully – rung by rung – he starts to climb the ladder. At the top of the ladder is a gallery. Mark moves along the maze of bridges until he is nearly above the Policemen.

Mark raises his head cautiously – and looks down.

Far below we can see the Inspector standing next to the Doctor – a tall, silver haired man – who is peering into an open trunk. Detectives are photographing the set. Mark raises his cine-camera . . . its gentle purring seems to echo round the studio.

CLOSE SHOT *of Mark's jacket pocket . . . A row of pencils is sticking out . . . As he leans forward the pencils tilt . . .*

Through the finder-matte of Mark's camera we see the Inspector – very far away – peering into the trunk and nodding.

A faint echo of conversation is overlaid –

> DOCTOR
> (*off-screen*)
> – no doubt at all . . . wounds were caused by the same instrument . . .

Mark changes lens (and alters the finder to a 75mm lens). The Doctor's face – thin and impersonal – appears in the finder over the lid of the trunk.

> – both women . . . subjected to the most violent shock . . .

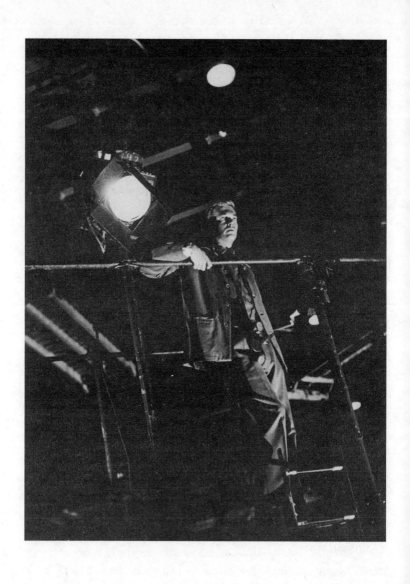

INSPECTOR
(*off-screen*)
What sort of shock?

DOCTOR
– still cannot determine – but look –!

He points to something in the trunk – out of the camera's eye-line . . .

CLOSE SHOT *of Mark.*

He balances carefully – then raises the camera above his head. As he leans forward, the pencils fall. We see them shooting like small torpedoes into the darkness below. They make three separate landings . . .

CLOSE SHOT *of the Inspector. Looking up.*

From his POV we see tiers of scaffolding deep in shadow . . .

INSPECTOR
Quiet, everyone. Please . . .

The Detectives make as much noise to become quiet as the normal occupants of the studio – and then there is complete silence.

Complete, except for the Doctor's asthmatic breathing . . . And then – so gently that it might almost be in our own minds – we hear a purring sound from the shadows above. The Inspector listens intently . . .

DETECTIVE
I thought I heard a putty cat!

There is a burst of laughter – the Inspector frowns.

INSPECTOR
I don't want to spoil anyone's fun, but we do have a maniac on our hands, and if we don't get him quickly there'll be a third unsolved murder to report to the Commissioner. So let's hurry things up, shall we?

DETECTIVE
Sorry, Chief!

The 'putty cat' Detective raises his flashlamp towards the trunk counter. In the brilliant flash of light that ensues, we glimpse a shadowy figure

121

moving towards a ladder high in the scaffolding . . . But then we are looking for it – no one else is. The flashlight dies away.

The scene fades with it.

CLOSE SHOT *of a knitting-needle held upwards.*

Another knitting-needle scales down it like a fireman descending a ladder . . . Camera pulls back.

INT. HELEN'S SITTING ROOM. DAY

Mrs Stephens is doing her knitting. The inevitable glass stands on the table beside her. Helen is seated opposite, reading from a newspaper.

> HELEN
> – she was appearing in Arthur Baden's new film *The Walls Are Closing In*, starring Diane Ashley –

CLOSE SHOT *of Mrs Stephens listening intently.*

> – a spokesman at the studio said that her performance in the film showed such promise, that her role was to have been built up . . . All work at the studio ceased today as a tribute to her memory! . . .

Mrs Stephens sips from her glass.

The Prime Minister to visit Athens.

> MRS STEPHENS
> Mark is in films, isn't he?

> HELEN
> Yes, darling . . . It is reliably –

> MRS STEPHENS
> I wonder if he knew her –

CLOSE SHOT *of Helen looking up.*

> HELEN
> I'll ask him tonight . . .

> MRS STEPHENS
> Is he taking you out?

HELEN

If he's free –

MRS STEPHENS

That's very chivalrous of him. Where's he taking you?

HELEN

I've no idea – and I don't suppose he has . . .

MRS STEPHENS

Which studio does he work at?

HELEN

I'll ask him –

MRS STEPHENS

If he's free –

Behind her back we see that her fingers are crossed.

HELEN

I'll bring him in and introduce you if –

MRS STEPHENS

I feel I know him –

HELEN

Now how can you –?

Mrs Stephens stiffens suddenly.

MRS STEPHENS

He's here –

CLOSE SHOT *of the window.*

Mark is standing outside – looking in.

Why don't we make him a present of the window? He
practically lives there –

*Helen beckons to Mark to come in . . . We see him nod eagerly – and
leave the window.*

HELEN

How did you know where he was standing?

MRS STEPHENS

The back of my neck told me . . . the part that I talk out of!

Helen hurries to the door of the sitting room.

INT. HALL. DAY

Mark closes the front door behind him . . . From his POV we see the door of Helen's sitting room open – and she stands on the threshold.

HELEN

Hallo . . .

MARK

Free?

HELEN

Yes –

MARK

Good! So am I . . .

HELEN

I'd like you to come in for a moment – and meet my mother.

MARK

Yes, please . . .

She holds open the door . . . He goes inside.

The screen suddenly greys out into the veiled images of Mrs Stephens' world. We hear Helen's voice.

HELEN
(*off-screen*)

Darling, this is Mark . . . Mark, my mother.

We hear the sound of footsteps shuffling shyly forward – and then Mark's voice, every intake of breath magnified.

MARK
(*off-screen*)

How do you do . . . Mrs Stephens . . .

We hear the pounding of someone's heart – and then Mrs Stephens' voice.

MRS STEPHENS
(*off-screen*)

Hallo, Mark –

As her voice dies away –

FADE IN:

INT. HELEN'S SITTING ROOM

CLOSE SHOT *of Mark's hand clasping Mrs Stephens'.*

CLOSE SHOT *of Mark looking at her, fascinated.*

From Mark's POV we see the sightless eyes turned towards his . . . Mrs Stephens' other hand gently feels the surface of his.

MRS STEPHENS
Have you been running, young man?

MARK
Yes –
(*he hesitates*)
– didn't want to be late for Helen –

HELEN
Thank you, Mark – You deserve a drink for that! What would you like?

MARK
Nothing – thank you . . . very much . . .

Mrs Stephens grunts, and reaches for her glass.

HELEN
Darling, I've left your supper in the –

MRS STEPHENS
Tell me young man . . . Which studio do you work at?

The screen greys out. We hear Mark's tiny intake of breath.

MARK
(*off-screen*)
Chipperfield Studio . . .

And that poor girl . . . where did she work?

Someone's heart is pounding fast.

> HELEN
> (*off-screen*)

At Brookwood –

> MRS STEPHENS

We were wondering if you knew her?

> MARK

No – No, I didn't . . .

> MRS STEPHENS

A pity. I do like first-hand information –

We hear Mark's small attempt at a laugh.

Oh, well – I mustn't keep you gossiping after you've run all
the way from – Where?

Again that little intake of breath.

> MARK

The station –

FADE OUT:

FADE IN:

*Mrs Stephens and Mark are staring at each other as if she has sight and
he hasn't. From Helen's POV we can see only Mark's back and her
mother's upturned face . . .*

> HELEN

Darling, may I tell you about your supper?

> MRS STEPHENS

No . . . go and be told about yours –
> (*she takes Mark's hand*)

Goodbye, Mark . . . I expect we shall meet again –

> MARK

I hope so – Goodbye . . .

(he turns to the door)

CLOSE SHOT *of Helen kissing her mother and whispering into her ear.*

> HELEN
>
> Darling, we forgot to toss –

Mrs Stephens grunts.

> Supper's laid out in the kitchen –

> MRS STEPHENS
>
> If you're not back early, you'll find me laid out with it!

> HELEN
>
> We'll be early! Good night, darling –

> MRS STEPHENS
>
> Good night . . .

Mark holds the door open for Helen and she goes into the passage . . .
Mark turns and takes a long look at Mrs Stephens. She is in the middle
of raising her glass . . . She stops suddenly, the glass poised mid-air . . .
He goes out – closing the door. She finishes her drink as if it is her last.

INT. PASSAGE. DAY

Helen is waiting by the door . . .

From her POV we see Mark coming eagerly towards her, his camera
over his shoulder.

> HELEN
>
> Mark . . .

> MARK
>
> Yes, Helen?

> HELEN
>
> I want to ask you something rather personal . . .

He looks at her anxiously.

> How long is it since you've gone out without that?

> MARK
>
> Without what?

128

HELEN

Your camera . . .

MARK

Oh . . .

CLOSE SHOT *of Mark.*

I . . . don't think I know –

HELEN

Exactly. I've never seen you without it . . . but are you going
to need it tonight?

He looks at her in silence.

Well are you? And if so . . . shall I bring some work with me
too?

MARK

I'm not going to need it tonight!

HELEN

Good – then give it to me –

She holds out her hand . . . He looks at her, appalled.

– it'll be quite safe – I'll put it away for you –

MARK
(*in a whisper*)

No –

HELEN

Then take it upstairs – if you can't trust me with it . . .

CLOSE SHOT *of Mark.*

MARK

I trust you –

HELEN

Then look –

She opens the door of her bedroom – and turns on the light.

– let's put it in here –

129

INT. HELEN'S BEDROOM

She crosses to a cupboard and unlocks it, then turns round . . . He is standing hesitantly on the threshold.

HELEN

Come in – and see for yourself –

He looks slowly round the room, stares for a moment at the bed in the corner, but he won't cross the threshold. He stays outside.

We'll put it in here – and lock it.

MARK

This . . . was my mother's room –

HELEN

Was it, Mark? . . .

Again he stares at the bed . . .

I am being tactless, aren't I? . . . It's just that . . . I thought it was growing into an extra limb, and – but you bring it with you if you want to.

He takes off his camera – and holds it out to her.

Thank you . . .

She takes it from him, puts it into the cupboard, and locks it. Then offers him the key.

MARK

You –

HELEN

Thank you.

CLOSE SHOT *of Mark.*

MARK

I feel –

HELEN

Yes?

MARK

Can't describe it! Could only photograph it –

She laughs.

HELEN

Shall I tell you what I feel?

MARK

Yes –

HELEN

Famished!

MARK

Good!

They hurry towards the door . . .

DISSOLVE TO:

EXT. MARK'S HOUSE. DAY

They walk down the steps of the house.

MARK

There's a small place round the corner . . . It's awfully good
on Christmas Day.

HELEN

Is it?

MARK

Yes . . . there aren't too many open then.

HELEN

No – it sounds fun.

MARK

This way –

CLOSE SHOT *of Mark and Helen walking along by the side of the
house.*

HELEN

I adore new restaurants . . .

132

Suddenly Mark stands motionless . . . He is staring at something off camera.

    – especially when –

Her voice trails away . . . she is staring at Mark staring at something.

In the shadows, at the mouth of an alley, a young couple are kissing.

Mark stands motionless, staring at them. Automatically his hand reaches for his camera. Helen starts to speak – then looks at him in silence. The man glances round . . . Mark hurries away and Helen stares after him.

CLOSE SHOT *of Mark.*

He turns back – waiting for Helen.

From his POV we see Helen come slowly towards him. She looks at him searchingly for a long moment.

He manages – but only just – to meet her eyes.

> HELEN
> Where is this restaurant?

> MARK
> Round the corner . . .

> HELEN
> Come on then . . .

CLOSE SHOT *of Mark.*

> MARK
> Thank you –

They walk slowly down the street.

DISSOLVE TO:

CLOSE SHOT *of Mrs Stephens.*

> MRS STEPHENS
> Sorry, young man, Helen's out –

Camera pulls back.

INT. SITTING ROOM. EVENING

Tony is standing unhappily opposite Mrs Stephens.

> TONY
> Oh –

> MRS STEPHENS
> With Mark – from upstairs –

> TONY
> Oh –

> MRS STEPHENS
> You can stay and talk to me – if you like –

> TONY
> Well I –

MRS STEPHENS

Know much about films?

TONY

Well –

MRS STEPHENS

Of film studios?

TONY

No, I –

MRS STEPHENS

Where's Chipperfield Studios?

TONY

Chipperfield, I suppose . . .

MRS STEPHENS

There's a phone book outside . . . Look up the number, will you? And see if you can get it –

TONY

Certainly . . . and then I must go to my room –

MRS STEPHENS

Granted –

She lifts her glass, and sits, waiting as he crosses the room.

DISSOLVE TO:

INT. RESTAURANT. NIGHT

A small and very pleasant restaurant, almost full. Helen and Mark have a corner table. They are dining by candlelight, and there is a bottle of wine in the middle of the table.

As camera tracks towards them, Helen is laughing.

HELEN

I like this place! And this dinner!

CLOSE SHOT *of Mark.*

He has again won the Academy Award.

135

– thank you, Mark . . .

MARK

Are you ready to talk about your book?

HELEN

I'm ready to talk about you . . .

His face falls.

It won't take a second – and it's best to have it said –

Mark looks.

Carrying a camera is only one of your habits, isn't it, Mark?

He looks at her in silence.

CLOSE SHOT *of Helen.*

– when you stared at that couple, you were like the little boy on that film you showed me . . . looking over the wall at something he shouldn't see. But Mark – you're strong enough now to lift that child off the wall . . . aren't you?

He hesitates.

– aren't you?

MARK

I'll try to be.

HELEN

Will you, Mark? . . . Will you really?

MARK

Yes . . .

HELEN

Lecture finished . . .

A pause.

MARK

When your book's published – will you go on working in a library?

Yes, Mark . . . in case, one day, a child comes in and asks for it!

MARK

I'll come in –

HELEN

I'm not popular with my customers! They ask me for horror comics – and I take their sticky hands and drag them to where there are books!

CLOSE SHOT *of Helen.*

– and do you know, Mark, waiting for them to come in next time and *ask* for books . . . is as exciting . . . as a horror comic . . .

MARK

What does your magic camera photograph?

HELEN

People . . .

MARK

Yes? . . .

HELEN

It's owned by a little boy who is terrified of grown-ups . . . but when he looks in his magic camera he sees grown-ups as they were when they were children . . . and he isn't frightened any longer –

CLOSE SHOT *of Mark listening, engrossed.*

– and one day he gives his camera away to a little boy who is even more frightened of grown-ups than he was – and do you know what he finds?

The little boy opposite her shakes his head.

– that when he looks at grown-ups without his camera he can still see them as they were when they were children! And that means that he's grown up himself . . .

A moment's pause. She drinks her wine – shy, awaiting his reaction.

> MARK

What made you think of this story?

> HELEN

You did –

CLOSE SHOT *of Mark.*

> . . . I looked out of my window – and saw you going off to
> work carrying that camera like a little boy with a satchel . . .
> and an idea came . . . so thank you . . .

> MARK

I'd like to think . . . I was responsible . . . in some way . . .

> HELEN

Now what do I do about the photographs?

> MARK

Take 'em!

*He slams the table so violently that a lady nearby looks around . . .
then reaches for his camera.*

> Oh –

Helen smiles.

> There isn't a single face that doesn't look like a child's – not a
> single one – if you catch it at the right moment –

He turns around excitedly and sees her watching him.

> It would be a challenge! . . . Unlike anything I've
> photographed –

> HELEN

What have you photographed, Mark?

> MARK

Everything. But nothing I'd want children to see –

She looks at him curiously.

> But this would belong to them – and they'd know if it wasn't

138

right . . . Oh, Helen . . . I would like to find those faces for you . . . with you . . .

HELEN

Very well! Let's try!

He laughs excitedly . . . She looks regretfully at her watch. At once he looks at his.

MARK

You made a promise to your mother –

HELEN
(*gently*)

Yes, Mark . . .

MARK

You'd better keep it –

HELEN

Thank you . . .

He signals to the head waiter . . . and pays his first bill for two . . .

DISSOLVE TO:

EXT. STREET. NIGHT

They walk along the street very close together, but not quite touching. Above them a light is shining on a blind revealing a shadow of a woman undressing . . .

Mark glances at the blind – then looks away quickly.

He stares ahead of him . . . and continues to stare ahead of him.

Suddenly Helen tucks her arm through his, and smiles up at him . . . they walk on in silence.

DISSOLVE TO:

INT. HALL OF MARK'S HOUSE. NIGHT

Helen and Mark come in quietly, and close the door.

She glances round the dimly lit hall . . . There is no light under any of the doors, except one at the end of the passage . . .

                    HELEN
        Mother must have gone to bed –
                    (*she turns to find him looking at her*)
        Mark, it was a wonderful evening . . .

                    MARK
        That's what I was going to say . . . a wonderful evening . . .

                    HELEN
                    (*gently*)
        And you made it wonderful . . . without your camera –

A shadow passes over his face.
                    (*gently*)
        I'll get it for you –

He stands motionless as she goes into her room . . .

From his POV we see the half-opened door – and the bed in the corner.

CLOSE SHOT *of Mark forcing himself to look away.*

Helen reappears on the threshold – the camera in her hand. He looks down at it – then slowly stretches out his hand.

        I wonder how this sees grown-ups –
                    (*she turns the camera round*)
        – me, for instance . . . now that I am one –
                    (*she looks at herself in the lens*)

                    MARK
    Not you –
                    (*he takes the camera from her*)

                    HELEN
    Mark –

                    MARK
    It never will . . . see you –

                    HELEN
    Why not?

                    140

He hesitates.

MARK

Whatever I photograph –

HELEN

Yes?

MARK

I always – lose . . .

HELEN

I don't understand.

The door at the end of the passage opens and Tony emerges in his dressing-gown, carrying a towel. He avoids looking at them – goes into the bathroom opposite, and slams the door.

He'll wake Mother –

There is the sound of running water.

– thank you, again, for my evening –
   (*she is standing very close to him, smiling up into his face*)
Will you go to bed now – and not stop up watching those films?

MARK

Well . . . I've a little work to do . . . then I'll go to bed . . . and think of how to find faces for you . . .

He looks down at the face which he has found for himself. She raises her head slowly.

. . . faces which – are faces which . . .

She kisses him very gently on the mouth.

The bathroom begins to sound like a small waterfall.

HELEN

Good night, Mark . . .

He watches her as she goes into the room, and closes the door. A light goes on beneath the door.

He stands very still for a moment . . . then turns the camera round and points the lens towards his lips.

Then he turns abruptly, and hurries up the stairs.

The waterfall cascades on.

The screen grows dark – and the dark-room grows out of it . . .

INT. DARK-ROOM. NIGHT

The big drying drum is turning, feeding the dry print into a box. A small motor drives it.

CLOSE SHOT *of the box. Mark is spooling up the film as it comes off the drier. Once or twice he can't help glancing at an image.*

CLOSE UP *of Vivian's face, in the image.*

Mark stops the motor and the drum, loosens the end of the film, spools up with a snap, slides the spool off and hurries out with it.

Mark hurries to his projector, threads the film and starts the projector. He flicks it on, as if it were a gramophone, then looks eagerly at the 16mm screen.

Behind him something moves in the shadows –

REVERSE SHOT *of Mark.*

Over the shoulder of someone who is standing deep in the shadows we see Mark. His head obscures what he is watching on the screen.

He turns round suddenly –

From Mark's POV we see the processing sinks deep in shadow. He starts to move towards them, then suddenly stares at the shadows at the back of the room.

Silence – except for the whirring of the 16mm projector.

CLOSE SHOT *of Mark's hand – switching on the light.*

Mark turns round . . . he is as astonished at what he sees as he can be.

Camera pans in its own good time to the back of the room.

Mrs Stephens is standing in the shadows . . . a heavy hand rests on a heavy stick . . . the sightless eyes stare unerringly towards the light switch.

MRS STEPHENS

Good evening, Mark . . .

MARK

. . . how did you – ?

MRS STEPHENS

The young man bathing himself brought me to your door . . . I managed the rest of the adventure alone . . .

He stands motionless, staring at her standing motionless.

Above her head an ancient, half-blind camera also stares at her.

The only movement in the room is her smile.

This is *one* room I expected to find locked –

MARK

I was never allowed a key . . . can't get used to them –

Mrs Stephens' sightless eyes stare at him.

I brought her home early –

CLOSE SHOT *of her hand – tightening on the heavy stick.*

MRS STEPHENS

Thank you . . .

MARK

Is there something you –

MRS STEPHENS

– a talk –

MARK

Next door would be more –

MRS STEPHENS

I'm at home here . . . I visit this room every night –

MARK

Visit?

MRS STEPHENS

The blind always live in the rooms they live under . . .

Mark nods.

Every night you pace for hours above my head! Why?

MARK

I've no one to talk to . . . in the rooms I live over . . .

Mrs Stephens nods. Her hand touches the black cloth loading bag, lying on the table.

MRS STEPHENS

I'm told that you stare too much . . . so do I –

CLOSE SHOT *of her hand – touching the black cloth bag.*

CLOSE SHOT *of Mark – walking slowly towards her.*

At once she raises the heavy stick – pointing it towards him.

CLOSE SHOT *of the stick. It is a shooting stick – with a sharp spike on the end of it, similar to the tripod on Mark's camera.*

Mark stares at the stick, fascinated.

CLOSE SHOT *of Mrs Stephens – exploring the inside of the black cloth bag with her free hand.*

Cloth . . . with something hard inside it . . .

MARK

It's a changing bag . . . we put films in it – so that the light won't spoil them . . .

MRS STEPHENS

How odd – that the light can spoil anything . . .

The screen greys out.

In Mrs Stephens' own dark-room we hear the hum of Mark's projector – and the pounding of Mark's heart – and, very faintly, the sounds of Tony bathing himself.

Every night you switch on that film machine –

We hear his tiny intake of breath.

What are these films you can't wait to look at?

The sound of his footsteps softly approaching.

MARK
(*off-screen*)

Like a chair?

MRS STEPHENS
(*off-screen*)

What is the film you're showing now?

Very faintly we hear Tony singing in his bath.

FADE IN:

The singing dies away, and the sound returns to normal.

Over Mark's shoulder we see Mrs Stephens holding her stick in front of her.

Why don't you lie to me? I'd never know . . .

MARK

You'd know at once –

Mrs Stephens smiles – then turns her head towards the 16mm screen.

MRS STEPHENS

Take me to your cinema –

MARK

Yes –

He takes her arm gently and guides her towards us –

Both of them stare at the 16mm screen . . . She leans forward – her face only inches from the screen – the light from the projector flickering on to her.

REVERSE ANGLE SHOT *of Mrs Stephens. Slowly she stretches out her hands and touches the screen . . .*

MRS STEPHENS

What am I seeing, Mark?

Her head and shoulders blot out most of the screen – but between her outspread fingers we catch a glimpse of a girl's terrified eyes.

Why don't you answer?

CLOSE SHOT *of Mark and Mrs Stephens.*

MARK
(staring at the screen)
It's no good – I was afraid it wouldn't be.

MRS STEPHENS

What?

MARK

The lights failed too soon.

MRS STEPHENS

They always do.
(pause)

MARK

I'll have to try again –

He hurries to his cine-camera.

MRS STEPHENS

I've yet to meet an artist who could judge his own work . . .

Mark slips a new spool of film into his cine-camera.

What do you think you've spoiled?

MARK

An opportunity . . . now I must find another –

He looks at her thoughtfully, then presses a light switch. A spotlight falls blindingly on to her eyes. He presses another switch, and then another, until the whole of her face is shining with light . . .

MRS STEPHENS

Why are you putting those lights on my face?

He walks towards her . . . She starts to back away . . .

The shadow of Mark's head appears on the 16mm screen. We see him raise his camera – then pull down the tripod.

Black out into the grey darkness of Mrs Stephens' world.

We hear the purring of Mark's camera – more clearly than we have yet heard it. (There is the faint rasp of a cog which needs oiling.) The sound of footsteps approaching . . . the purring changes direction . . .

MRS STEPHENS
(off-screen)

Mark –

MARK
(off-screen)

It's almost over . . .

The purring is on top of her . . . There is a sudden thud . . .

FADE IN:

Mrs Stephens is leaning against the wall . . . she has dropped her heavy stick. It lies on the floor a few feet away from her. Mark is kneeling in front of her – the tripod firmly on the floor. The cine-camera is pointing upwards into her face. He peers excitedly into the viewfinder.

Please let me finish! It's for Helen!

She edges towards her stick. He hurries forward and picks it up . . . He looks at the spike on the end of it – then carefully gives it to her by the handle. She grasps it tightly.

MRS STEPHENS

What do you mean? It's for Helen?

MARK

She wants to see something I've photographed!

He returns excitedly to his camera.

MRS STEPHENS

My daughter sees enough of my face without photographs . . .

On Mark's focusing screen we see the fear on her face . . . Her hand trembles as she wipes away the perspiration.

147

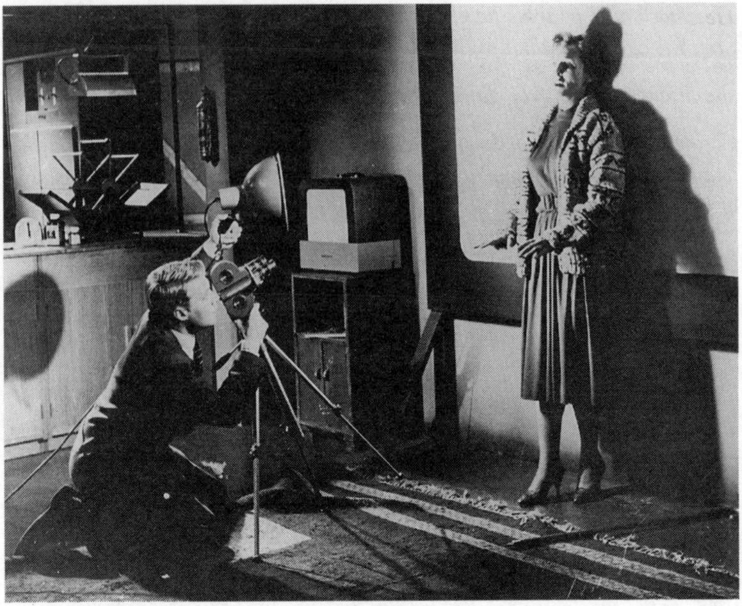

MARK
(*off-screen*)

Please . . . don't be frightened –

MRS STEPHENS

Not frightened! Hot!

But it is fear that we are looking at.

So put that camera away . . .

On the focusing screen we see her moisten her lips nervously.

MARK

Yes!

He switches off the camera abruptly, and folds up the tripod. He turns away without looking at her – and hurries to the door.

CLOSE SHOT *of Mrs Stephens listening to his movements – puzzled.*

MRS STEPHENS

In rather a hurry, aren't you?

He glances towards her.

From his POV we see the fear in her eyes . . . He looks away at once, staring into the darkened room.

MARK

It's late –

From her POV (shooting over her shoulder with a large CLOSE SHOT of her ear in the foreground) we see Mark standing in the doorway – and hear, very clearly, his quick, uneasy breathing.

You must be tired . . .

MRS STEPHENS

You're anxious to get rid of me all of a sudden.

We hear his quick intake of breath.

I won't be selfish . . . You can take some more pictures – if you want to . . .

MARK

No . . . thank you –

MRS STEPHENS
(quietly)

Why not, Mark?

MARK

Run out of film –

MRS STEPHENS

Can't you find some – to please Helen?

He glances towards her – then hurries into the next room.

You don't trust yourself to take any more, do you?

INT. MARK'S SITTING ROOM. NIGHT

The tapping of her stick is overlaid. Mark hurries to the door and opens it – staring into the dimly lit passage. Over his shoulder we see her tapping her way towards him from the dark-room . . .

149

Instinct's a wonderful thing, isn't it Mark? A pity it can't be photographed –

Over her shoulder we follow the stick towards him.

– if I'd listened to it years ago, I might have kept my sight –
                    (*she approaches the door*)
I wouldn't have let a man operate I had no faith in . . . so I'm listening to it now . . .
                    (*she puts her face close to him*)
It says all this filming isn't healthy – and that you need help –

His face is averted . . . his eyes are closed.

– get it, Mark . . . get it quickly . . . and *until* you've got it . . . I don't want you and Helen to see each –

MARK

I'll never photograph her . . . I promise you that –

MRS STEPHENS

I'd rather you don't have the chance –

He turns towards her – a small boy who suddenly understands what contagious means . . .

I mean it, Mark. And if you don't listen to me . . . one of us will move from this house – which would be a pity, because we'd never find a cheaper . . .

MARK

You'll never have to move . . . because of me . . . I promise you –

MRS STEPHENS

Good boy –
                    (*she takes his hand*)
The stairs are the difficult part . . .

They go into the passage.

INT. PASSAGE. NIGHT

He guides her gently down the stairs . . . Over their shoulders we can see the door of Helen's room.

MRS STEPHENS

Far enough, Mark . . .

He stares at Helen's room – then looks quickly away. Suddenly she raises her hands – and runs them gently over his face . . .

MARK

– taking my picture?

MRS STEPHENS

Yes . . .

We can see his eyes through her outstretched fingers.

MARK

It's been a long time . . . since anyone did –

MRS STEPHENS

Mark . . . what's troubling you?

MARK

Good night, Mrs Stephens.

He turns away abruptly and hurries up the stairs.

MRS STEPHENS

   – you'll have to –

She looks towards Helen's room – then turns slowly towards her own.

HIGH ANGLE SHOT *of Mrs Stephens opening the door of her room – and Mark opening the door of his.*

   DISSOLVE TO:

CLOSE SHOT *of a bottle of whisky standing by a bedside.*

INT. MRS STEPHENS' BEDROOM. NIGHT

She is lying in bed, staring at the ceiling . . . We hear footsteps moving overhead.

Camera pans to the window . . . It is dark.

   DISSOLVE TO:

CLOSE SHOT *of the same bottle of whisky – now almost empty. Mrs Stephens' heavy breathing is overlaid.*

Camera pans to the window. It is daybreak.

The footsteps are still moving about above; things are being dragged across the floor.

   DISSOLVE TO:

CLOSE SHOT *of Helen in a dressing-gown looking out of a window.*

INT. HELEN'S ROOM. MORNING

From Helen's POV we see Mark hurrying down the street, his camera over his shoulder.

   DISSOLVE TO:

CLOSE SHOT *of the Inspector looking out of a window.*

INT. DON JARVIS' OFFICE. MORNING

From his POV we see Mark hurrying along the studio quadrangle, his camera over his shoulder. He is one of a crowd of people scurrying towards their jobs. Camera pulls back – Don Jarvis is seated at his desk.

Arthur Baden and the Chief Publicity Man are seated in front of him.
The Sergeant stands by the door.

JARVIS

Have you any suspicions, Chief Inspector?

INSPECTOR

It could be any of them . . .

SERGEANT

That's the trouble with film people – they're all peculiar –
(*hastily*)
– present company excepted –

He catches a glare from the great man.

PUBLICITY MAN

Speaking of peculiar people –

The Inspector turns round.

We've a psychiatrist coming down today. Dr Rosen –

INSPECTOR

I know him.

PUBLICITY MAN

It's pure publicity – and I promise he won't do any work –

INSPECTOR

What *will* he do?

PUBLICITY MAN

Get himself photographed . . . We're telling the press he's
here to help the case – and to see if he can spot the
murderer –

SERGEANT

And the best of luck –

JARVIS

Do you object, Chief Inspector?

INSPECTOR

No –

The Publicity Man sighs with relief.

I'll be frank. I'd welcome anyone's help . . . I don't know how this maniac kills – or why he kills – or who he'll kill next, but if he isn't caught quickly –
> (*he shrugs*)

BADEN

Inspector, have you convinced yourself he's a member of my unit?

INSPECTOR

No, sir . . . but a few things seem to point to it . . . No one outside your unit admits to knowing the girl . . . There was a trunk all ready for her . . . and with the risks he was running, I think he'd have to use surroundings he was familiar with . . . Where is your unit now?

BADEN

Waiting for me on the set –

INSPECTOR

I'd like to watch them at their jobs, sir. It may tell me more than a hundred interviews –

BADEN

But, Inspector, the strain on them is already –

JARVIS

Come now, Arthur, if that's what the Inspector wants –

INSPECTOR

I'm afraid it is, sir . . . now where could I get the best view?

BADEN
(*sulkily*)

On the dolly . . . the camera . . . You can watch everyone and everything from there . . . including me –

INSPECTOR

Very well, sir . . . I'll become a member of your camera crew –

BADEN
(*to Don Jarvis*)
– if the unions don't object –

DISSOLVE TO:

INT. STAGE E

A member of the camera crew places his cine-camera and lunch bag on a shelf. Snatches of whispered conversations are overlaid –

VOICE I
I hear they're making an arrest today –

VOICE 2
– hope it's D.J. It's about time they caught up with him –

Mark turns round and walks towards the small group of people assembled round the studio camera –

DISSOLVE TO:

CLOSE SHOT *of a book entitled* The Art of Fly Fishing.

INT. CAR. DAY

Through the windscreen we see the entrance to the studio. The driver glances round at his passenger whose face is completely obscured by the book . . . All we can see is a shock of white hair protruding above it . . .

DRIVER
We're there, Doctor –
(*to Sergeant on gate*)
Dr Rosen!

DOCTOR
What a pity –

He continues reading.

The car enters the studio.

DISSOLVE TO:

INT. STAGE E. DAY

The (studio) camera is ready for a tracking shot. The set is redressed as the Hat Department of the store. The Inspector stands on the dolly, looking round with interest.

The Doctor is sitting in a chair watching everything like an excited schoolboy. The Sergeant has positioned himself near the sound crew.

Baden walks on to the set, his arm round Diane's shoulder. He is talking to her softly. She keeps her eyes on the floor; he leads her to the front of the studio camera . . .

> BADEN
> Try it, darling . . . We'll all be with you –

He pats her arm reassuringly . . . The Chief Cameraman nods to Mark.

From the Inspector's POV we see Mark pull a tape measure from the front of the camera and hold it to Diane's forehead. From Mark's POV we see the Inspector watching him over the top of the studio camera. A man with a shock of white hair is also watching him . . . and the Sergeant stares at him from the other side of the set. The tape measure in Mark's hand remains steady . . .

From the Inspector's POV we see Mark replace the tape measure and take up his position on a small stool by the side of the camera.

> ASSISTANT DIRECTOR
> (*shouting*)
> Quiet, everyone. Let's run it –

The Doctor sneezes violently – and all heads turn towards him.

> DOCTOR
> Terribly sorry –

In the nervous laughter that follows, the Assistant Cameraman whispers to the Chief Cameraman.

> ASSISTANT CAMERAMAN
> That sneezer geezer's a psychiatrist! . . . Heard it on the grapevine –

CLOSE SHOT *of Mark turning round to look at the Doctor – a hint of hope in his face.*

CLOSE SHOT *of the Inspector following Mark's glance.*

> ASSISTANT DIRECTOR
> (*shouting*)
> All right, everyone – let's run it . . .

Over the Inspector's shoulder we track towards the rehearsal . . . We see Mark swing out into space on his stool, turning the handle of the focus-puller. Diane approaches the hat counter. The Assistant smiles at her . . .

> DIANE
> I'd like to see . . . that one . . .

The Assistant hands her a hat. Diane tries it on.

> – have you it . . . in red . . . ?

> ASSISTANT
> Certainly, madam.

> DIANE
> – in . . . red . . .
> (*suddenly she covers her face in her hands*)
> I can't – I can't – Arthur –

She bursts into tears and runs off the set. From the Inspector's POV we see Baden whisper to the Assistant Director – then hurry after Diane.

> ASSISTANT DIRECTOR
> Ten minutes break, everyone –

The unit dissolves into small, chattering groups. The Assistant Director hurries up to the Doctor.

> Can you suggest anything, Doctor?

> DOCTOR
> No. It looked jolly interesting to me . . .

> ASSISTANT DIRECTOR
> I mean to help her psychologically –

DOCTOR

Yes. Give the girl a proper rest . . . Ten minutes is useless!

ASSISTANT DIRECTOR
(*hastily*)

Thank you, Doctor –

He bustles off and the Doctor is left alone. He glances round thoughtfully . . .

From the Doctor's POV we see the small, chattering groups . . . Then we see Mark standing a few yards away, watching him. The Doctor smiles at him pleasantly.

DOCTOR

What's *your* job?

MARK

I'm a focus-puller . . .

DOCTOR

Oh . . . so am I, in a way.

MARK

I was wondering if you knew my father – Professor Lewis . . .

DOCTOR

Professor . . . but of course I knew him. He lectured to me –

He looks at Mark with renewed interest. So does the Inspector.

From his POV we see Mark and the Doctor talking . . . The Doctor is fidgeting with his watch chain . . . Mark fidgets with his jacket button. The Inspector then glances towards the Hat Salesman, who is holding court in the corner. We return to Mark and the Doctor.

– he was an extraordinary man – quite brilliant –

MARK

You know what he was interested in before he died?

DOCTOR

No? Tell me –

Mark puts his hands behind his back.

MARK

I don't remember what he called it . . . It was something to
do with what causes people to be . . . peeping Toms . . .

DOCTOR

Scoptophilia! . . . That would interest him! A most fertile
mind –

MARK

Scopto –?

DOCTOR

– philia . . . The morbid urge to gaze . . . Coined since his
day . . . Have you any manuscripts of his which I could –?

MARK

He thought . . . it could be cured . . .

DOCTOR

Usually. Now about his manuscripts –

MARK

Quickly –?

DOCTOR

The cure? Very quick . . . A couple of years analysis – three
times a week – an hour a time – and it's soon up-rooted . . .

CLOSE SHOT *of Mark – his last hope gone.*

– if you've any of his papers on the subject?

MARK

Yes, Doctor . . .

DOCTOR

I'd like to see them – I'll give you my address, young man –

*From the Sergeant's POV we see the Doctor hand Mark a card, and
pat him jovially on the shoulder. The Sergeant edges up to the Inspector.*

SERGEANT

Wonder what all that's about?

INSPECTOR

We'll find out afterwards . . . Now, listen . . . I want you to watch who brings their own lunches . . . Someone ate home-made cakes and sandwiches by the side of those bushes – and we may get a lead –

                    SERGEANT
Right, sir –

Camera pans to a shelf in the corner . . . A lunch basket stands next to a cine-camera.

DISSOLVE TO:

We hear the Assistant Director call out:

                ASSISTANT DIRECTOR
We're stopping at four today – so have a quick lunch, everyone! Back at two sharp!

FADE IN *on the lunch basket.*

Overlaid is the noise of the unit dispersing. Mark picks up his camera – then reaches for the lunch basket. An urgent voice whispers behind him . . .

                    VOICE
Hey, Mark –

He turns round. The Clapper Boy is standing there . . . The Clapper Boy glances round carefully . . . The Inspector and Sergeant are wandering casually towards the door.

                CLAPPER BOY
Can't wait to show you this!
            (*bringing out a small postcard*)
I ought to charge you –!

He winks at Mark, gives him the postcard.

CLOSE SHOT *of the postcard. We see Milly's face and naked shoulders framed between Mark's hands . . .*

                CLAPPER BOY
                (*off-screen*)
You don't get that in *Sight and Sound* – Isn't she terrific? . . . Got some more – if you're interested –

Mark hands it back.

                          MARK

You've given me . . . an idea . . .

                    CLAPPER BOY

I'll bet I have!

Mark turns towards the exit.

    Hey! Where are you going?

                          MARK

Phone – may be my last chance – and . . . thanks –

                    CLAPPER BOY

But your lunch –

                          MARK

You have it! . . .

He hurries excitedly towards the exit . . .

CLOSE SHOT *of the Clapper Boy staring at his photograph.*

                    CLAPPER BOY

– some photograph! Well lit too!

He reaches for the lunch basket, then walks towards the exit where the Sergeant is waiting casually.

    CUT TO:

INT. CAMERA ROOM

Mark is talking at a coin-box telephone.

                          MARK

Can't manage Saturday, sir, but they're letting us off early
today! This afternoon – after work – may be my last chance –

While Mark is talking he is scribbling on a form. He has some more pennies ready for the coin-box.

    CROSS CUT TO:

INT. NEWSAGENT'S SHOP. DAY

                    MR PETERS
        – be here at six o'clock. Milly'll be waiting –

                    MARK
        Six o'clock . . .

                    MR PETERS
        On the dot, Mark, or she'll go –

                    MARK
        I'll be there, sir –

                    MR PETERS
        You'd better be!

INT. CAMERA ROOM

Mark rings off. He is smiling. He puts in another 4d and dials a number. His pen is poised over the form he is filling in.

                    MARK
        Hallo? Is that the Public Library? . . . You have a Miss Helen
        Stephens employed there? Yes . . . can you tell me if her
        name is spelt with a V or a PH, I want to send her a tic–PH?
        . . . Thank you.

We see the form is a last will and testament.

        I, Mark Lewis, etc., etc., leave, etc., etc., to Miss Helen Ste–
        ens all my worldly goods, etc.

He fills in PH . . .

INT. CAMERA ROOM

The door bursts open and the Clapper Boy appears.

                    CLAPPER BOY
        They're waiting!

        CUT TO:

THE SET. DAY

CLOSE SHOT *of Dr Rosen smiling.*

> DOCTOR ROSEN
>
> He asked if I knew his father . . . which I did . . . a brilliant man –

EXT. GROUNDS OF STUDIO. DAY

The Inspector and Doctor are standing by the bushes where Mark and Vivian met.

> INSPECTOR
>
> Is that all he wanted?

> DOCTOR
>
> I think so . . . we had a little chat about scoptophilia – and he's going to show me –

> INSPECTOR
>
> About what?

> DOCTOR
>
> Voyeurism –

> INSPECTOR
>
> Eh?

> DOCTOR
>
> What makes people into Peeping Toms, one of his father's subjects, apparently –

> INSPECTOR
> (*slowly*)
>
> Peeping Toms . . .

> DOCTOR
>
> An interesting boy . . . he has his father's eyes . . . you don't suspect him, do you?

> INSPECTOR
>
> I suspect 'em all – what about you?

DOCTOR

I'm interested in that chap with the bald head and hatchet face . . . there's something on his mind!

INSPECTOR

No wonder . . . he's the director –!

He turns away thoughtfully.

DISSOLVE TO:

CLOSE SHOT *of Mark glancing impatiently at his watch.*

INT. STUDIO. DAY

CLOSE SHOT *of Baden glancing at his watch . . . He whispers to the Assistant Director.*

ASSISTANT DIRECTOR

All right, everyone. This is the last shot . . . Make it a good one!

Camera pans to a corner of the studio.

The Inspector and Sergeant stand in the shadows.

INSPECTOR
(quietly)

Got your list, Sergeant?

SERGEANT

Yes, sir –

(he produces it)

INSPECTOR

I want to see how some of them spend their spare time . . .

SERGEANT

Which ones, sir?

INSPECTOR

Exactly, Sergeant –

(he looks round thoughtfully)

– which ones?

DISSOLVE TO:

164

CLOSE SHOT *of sign:* PUBLIC LIBRARY.

EXT. PUBLIC LIBRARY. DAY

LONG SHOT *of very modern, glass-walled building. Helen comes out with a manuscript in a parcel under her arm.*

EXT. PUBLIC LIBRARY. DAY

Mark watches her. Beyond him stands an insignificant-looking man in a raincoat.

EXT. LIBRARY

Helen looks at her watch.

EXT. LIBRARY

Mark looks at his.

INSERT: 5.45.

EXT. LIBRARY

Helen hurries homeward.

EXT. LIBRARY

Mark slowly turns his back and walks away, gradually gathering speed. The man in the raincoat follows him.

EXT. NEWSAGENT'S SHOP. LATE AFTERNOON

Mark hurries towards the shop . . . ahead of him a street clock stands at just on six. Mark unslings his cine-camera and photographs this clock . . . then he hurries into the shop.

The man in the raincoat walks into camera. He looks at the clock, puzzled, then glances at the newsagent's window. He gazes with interest at Mark's photograph of Milly, then walks thoughtfully down the street.

All the clocks in the kingdom chime the hour of six . . .

INT. NEWSAGENT'S SHOP. LATE AFTERNOON

Mr Peters is behind the counter.

> MR PETERS
>
> Don't make a habit of this –

> MARK
>
> I won't, sir –

> MR PETERS
>
> Milly's upstairs –

> MARK
>
> Right, sir –

He turns to the door.

> MR PETERS
>
> I've got to go out . . . If you finish before I'm back, lock up
> and put this through the letter-box . . .
> > (*he holds out a key*)

CLOSE SHOT *of Mark staring at the key.*

> What's the matter? Haven't you ever seen a key before?

Mark takes the key . . . He starts to smile.

> The till will be empty – if that's what you're smiling about –

Mark turns to the door.

> You know what I want now! No fancy stuff . . .

Mark goes into the inner room; he is still smiling.

DISSOLVE TO:

EXT. NEWSAGENT'S SHOP. LATE AFTERNOON

*From the opposite side of the street, we see Mr Peters locking the door of
the shop, and hurrying down the road. The man in the raincoat watches
him, puzzled.*

CLOSE SHOT *of Milly – very angry, in a dressing-gown.*

MILLY

You've spoiled my whole evening, you have –

INT. NEWSAGENT'S STUDIO. LATE AFTERNOON

Mark closes the door behind him.

MARK

Sorry, Milly –

MILLY

What's the idea?

MARK

I shan't be here tomorrow –
(*he hurries to the window*)

MILLY

Why? Going on manoeuvres with the boy scouts?

*He starts to draw the curtains – and stops suddenly . . . Over his
shoulder we see the man in the raincoat standing on the opposite side of
the street.*

MARK

I thought so!

Mark raises his cine-camera and carefully photographs the Detective through a chink in the curtains.

MILLY

Have you gone *absolutely* –

MARK

I'm just . . . completing a documentary –

MILLY

You're a document and a half, you are. Is it safe to be alone with you?

He draws the curtains – and turns round.

– might be more fun if it wasn't . . .

He turns round and walks slowly – and a little sadly – towards her . . .

BLACK OUT:

The screen remains dark for a moment.

FADE TO:

AN HOUR LATER. EARLY EVENING

From the Detective's POV, we see the chink of light between the curtains of a window above the newsagent's shop go out. Camera tracks towards the door of the shop. Mark comes out, his cine-camera over his shoulder. He has a key in his hand . . . He closes the door of the shop . . . then looks at the key. He fits it into the lock – then slips it through the letter-box. He turns and hails a taxi.

CLOSE SHOT *of the Detective. He looks at the shop, hesitates, decides to follow Mark – hails another cab.*

EXT. STREET

Mark gets into his taxi. As the driver pulls down the flag . . .

CUT TO:

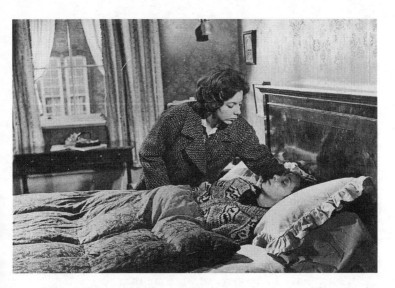

Mrs Stephens' head falling on to her chest.

INT. MRS STEPHENS' BEDROOM. EARLY EVENING

She is lying in bed – completely drunk – snoring lustily. A hand smooths her forehead.

Camera pulls back.

Helen is leaning over the bed. She has her coat on.

> HELEN
>
> Darling . . .

She shakes her mother's shoulders . . . Mrs Stephens snores on.

> Darling –

She shakes her again – but it is hopeless. Helen pulls the bedclothes round her mother, then turns away. She picks up a large envelope and her handbag, and hurries to the door.

INT. PASSAGE. MARK'S HOUSE. EARLY EVENING

Helen walks towards the stairs. The door of Tony's room opens, and he pokes his head round.

                        TONY
Hallo –

                        HELEN
Hallo, Tony . . .

                        TONY
Where are you going?

                        HELEN
To leave something for Mark . . .

                        TONY
You haven't much time for me these days –

                        HELEN
Tony –

                        TONY
It's all right – I'll be here – if you want me –
                    (*he turns to his room*)
– by the way . . . your mother was yelling out something
before you came in . . . about Mark photographing her –

                        HELEN
Photographing Mother? You must be mistaken!

                        TONY
Of course. See you sometime –

*He goes into his room, closing the door. She stares after him for a
moment, then hurries up the stairs.*

INT. PASSAGE BY MARK'S ROOM. DAY

Helen knocks on the door.

                        HELEN
Mark . . . ?

No answer. She knocks again, then opens the door and goes inside.

INT. MARK'S SITTING ROOM. EARLY EVENING

Helen enters and glances towards the door of the dark-room.

                        170

Mark?

No answer. She looks thoughtfully at the envelope in her hand – then goes in to the dark-room.

INT. MARK'S DARK-ROOM

Helen fumbles for a switch . . . she finds one and presses it . . . A spotlight falls on Mark's projector, throwing its shadow on to the dazzling white screen. Helen smiles, and walks towards the projector.

EXT. HOUSE. DAY

Taxi arrives and Mark gets out.

INT. POLICE PHONE BOOTH. EARLY EVENING

DETECTIVE

. . . don't know what to make of it, sir . . . He went to a library, a solicitor's office, and a newsagent's shop – private photography there, if you ask me. Shall I hang around outside the house, sir? Don't think so, either . . . All right, sir, I'll give you the details when I get back . . . Bye, sir.

(he replaces the receiver)

CLOSE SHOT *of Helen. She is standing by the projector, holding her envelope thoughtfully.*

INT. MARK'S DARK-ROOM

She smiles suddenly and opens her envelope. She takes out a bound manuscript . . . We see a label on the manuscript: The Magic Camera *by Helen Stephens. She takes a pencil from her pocket, and opens the manuscript. Then she sits at Mark's table and writes a note on the flyleaf. The projector is at her elbow . . .*

DISSOLVE TO:

A telephone by a man's elbow . . . It rings . . .

INT. SCOTLAND YARD. EVENING

The Chief Inspector snatches up the telephone.

> CHIEF INSPECTOR
> Chief Inspector Gregg! *What?* Put him on the line . . .

CROSS CUT TO:

Mr Peters – looking very sick – on the telephone.

> MR PETERS
> – went up to look around – found her –

CLOSE SHOT *of the Chief Inspector.*

> CHIEF INSPECTOR
> Yes, yes . . . What's the address? . . . *Newsagent's shop?* . . .
> Did you say news? –

He slams down the receiver, and jumps to his feet.

DISSOLVE TO:

EXT. ROAD. EVENING

*An empty taxi cruising down the street . . . It passes the Detective in the
raincoat walking away from Mark's house.*

DISSOLVE TO:

CLOSE SHOT *of a note on a flyleaf which reads 'From one Magic
Camera – which needs the help of Another'.*

INT. MARK'S DARK-ROOM. NIGHT

*Helen closes the manuscript and lays it carefully by the side of the
projector. She turns to leave – then looks curiously at the projector.*

CLOSE SHOT *of Helen – hesitating. Like a small girl in front of her
mother's make-up box, she touches the projector tentatively, hesitates
again, then presses a switch . . . A beam of light shoots out . . . We
watch Helen's face as she looks at the screen . . . Nothing seems wrong
for a few seconds – then something starts to happen to the corners of her
mouth . . . and then her eyes become locked . . . and cannot stop
watching . . . Some kind of sound comes from the back of her throat*

. . . Her hands dig into the table and she tries to stand up . . . She cannot manage it the first time – and keeps on watching, then, like a child waking from a nightmare, she jerks herself away from the table, and stumbles towards the door . . .

CLOSE SHOT *of Mark standing there – watching her . . .*

CLOSE SHOT *of Helen staring at him . . . again we hear that sound from the back of her throat . . . He looks away from her at once.*

> MARK
> Don't let me see you . . . frightened . . .
>> *(he pushes the door wide open . . .)*
> Leave –
>> *(he looks at her – then looks quickly away)*
> Hurry, Helen –

> HELEN
> Not . . .

> MARK
> *Leave –*

> HELEN
> Not . . .
>> *(she turns away from him and forces the words out)*
> . . . till I know . . .

> MARK
> Now –

She stands with her back to him . . . From REVERSE ANGLE *we see her struggling for breath. Over her shoulder we see him staring at the 16mm screen.*

> HELEN
> That film . . .

Over her shoulder we see him hurry towards the projector.

> That film . . .

The sound of him switching it off.

> . . . is . . . just a film . . .

She wheels round towards him.

. . . isn't it –?

From REVERSE ANGLE *we see her looking at him.*

. . . horrible . . . horrible . . . but . . . just a film . . . isn't it?

CLOSE SHOT *of Mark.*

MARK

No . . .
>   (*he walks towards the door*)
I killed them . . .
>   (*he locks the door with a hint of sadness*)
And now that you know . . . I want you with me . . . a while –

CLOSE SHOT *of Helen – not enough breath to scream . . . hardly
enough to breathe.*

You'll be safe – as long as I can't see you frightened – so
stand in the shadows, Helen . . . please . . .

She stands motionless.

. . . please . . .

*From her POV we see him standing in front of the door, looking ahead
of him . . . She backs slowly away into the shadows at the back of the
room . . .*

She's right . . . your mother . . . must tell someone everything
. . . sorry . . . has to be you –

CLOSE SHOT *of Helen standing in the shadows where her mother stood.*

This was his laboratory . . . and you know some of what he
did . . . but not all –

*The room is suddenly filled with the terrified screaming of a small boy.
Helen wheels round . . . The screaming seems to be coming from the
walls . . . Mark's hand is on a switch – one of a number on a panel.*

. . . aged five . . .

*He presses another switch . . . There is a click, and the screaming stops,
to be replaced by a low sobbing.*

. . . aged seven . . .

He presses another switch . . . There is a moment's silence.

– all the rooms were wired for sound . . . and . . . still are –

We suddenly hear the ticking of a clock.

Your room –

CLOSE SHOT *of Helen – listening.*

Your mother's –

The click of a switch – and we hear a loud snoring.

Tony's –

The click of a switch – and we hear Tony's voice.

> TONY
> (*off-screen*)

No one will come in . . . honestly, darling –

> GIRL'S VOICE
> (*off-screen*)

I don't care –

> TONY
> (*off-screen*)

But darling –

> GIRL'S VOICE
> (*off-screen*)

Stop it, Tony –

Mark listens with interest . . .

> HELEN
> (*quietly*)

Turn it off –

He does so – at once. She walks towards him . . . He turns away from her –

Look at me, Mark –

MARK

Not if you're frightened . . .

HELEN

Look at me –

Slowly he faces her . . .

What did you do . . . to those girls?

MARK

No.

HELEN

What did you do, Mark . . . ?

He tries to turn away – but she follows him.

If you want to torment me . . . for the rest of my life . . . then make me *imagine* –

CLOSE SHOT *of Mark – his eyes closed.*

What did you do . . . to those girls?

MARK

– I can't –

HELEN

Show me, Mark . . .

MARK

But if you're frightened . . .

HELEN

Show me – or I'll remain frightened . . . for the rest of my life. *Show me* –

He turns to his cine-camera, and picks it up . . . He releases the tripod . . .

Camera holds on Helen. She stands very still against the wall. Mark's voice is overlaid –

MARK
(off-screen)

Do you know . . . what the most frightening thing in the
world is? . . .

She is looking at something, puzzled.

It's fear.

The sound of his footsteps approaching . . .

So I did something . . . very simple –

We see a look of fear spring into her eyes.

Very simple.

*We see the spike approaching her throat . . . but she is looking at
something else.*

When they felt the spike . . . touching their throats . . . and
knew I was going to kill them . . .

The spike is touching her throat . . .

. . . I made them – watch their own deaths –

CLOSE SHOT *of Helen's face several times its natural size. She is
looking at herself in a large circular magnifying mirror which has
been fitted over the camera's face. The mirror entirely obscures both
Mark and the camera. There is a small hole in the mirror through
which the lens of the camera winks. As Helen looks at her terrified
distorted face this small hole gives her an extra eye in the middle of
her forehead . . .*

I made them see their own terror as the spike went in . . . and if
death has a face, they saw that too –

CLOSE SHOT *of Mark – crouching behind the mirror, sweat pouring
down his forehead . . . his finger on the trigger of the camera –*

Not you! Not you! I'll never photograph you! I promised – I
promised – Not you!

Helen's eyes are closed . . . The spike is still touching her throat.

CLOSE SHOT *of Mark – his face turned away from the viewfinder.*

HELEN

   . . . frightened . . . for you . . .

There's the sound of a car pulling up . . . He hurries to the other room.

EXT. HOUSE. NIGHT

The Police arrive: three cars.

Mark appears at an upstairs window with his camera.

SERGEANT

  Look out!

He thinks Mark has a gun. They all duck.

Mark raises his camera and photographs them.

The Police recover and charge for the house.

Mark disappears.

INT. DARK-ROOM. NIGHT

Mark hurries back into the room carrying his camera. He knows exactly what he has to do.

                              HELEN
Mark! Mark! Give yourself up!

                              MARK
I've been ready for this . . . for such a long time . . .

Rapidly he fixes his camera on to a hook on the wall . . . Then he adjusts the tripod so that the spikes protrude towards him . . .

                              HELEN
What are you –

                              MARK
It'll be all right –

He makes chalk marks on the floor in front of the camera, then switches on all the floodlights. We can hear the Policemen pounding on the door.

I can beat that –

He crosses to a switch – presses it . . . The room is filled with a small boy's screaming.

                              HELEN
Give yourself up . . . Mark –

He stands next to her, and looks at his long array of cameras. We see that each one of them has been fitted with a small metal disc (a delayed release), and that some of the older cameras have flashlights attached.

                              MARK
Watch them, Helen . . . Watch them say goodbye – one by one –
                    (*he presses a master switch on the wall*)
I've timed this . . . so often . . .

Slowly he walks past his cameras . . . As he does, the metallic disc on each one explodes with a little plop – and the eye of each camera winks once as if in salute. Some go off with flashlights on either side of the room. The sound of footsteps hurrying up the stairs . . .

*Ahead of Mark – coming steadily closer – are the spikes of the tripod
. . . The mirror on the cine-camera reflects the approach – and Helen's
terrified face.*

HELEN

No – No –

*The child's screaming reaches its peak as Mark approaches the spikes
. . . Ahead of him, on the small table where his projector stands, is
Helen's book* The Magic Camera.

MARK

I wish . . . I could have found your faces for you . . .

The Policemen are now rattling on the dark-room door.

Helen – I'm afraid –

*We see his face, terrified, in the magnifying mirror . . . The spikes are
against his throat . . . The eye of the camera is winking rapidly . . .*

I'm glad I'm afraid –

*Heavy shoulders are pressing against the dark-room door . . . as it breaks
in, Mark lunges forward against the spikes . . . The cine-camera is
wrenched away from the wall as he falls back . . . He crashes against the
small table, which falls over . . . He is not parted from his camera – it is
fixed to him by the tripod, and falls back with him, covering his face like
a canopy . . . We see his face in the lens of the cine-camera . . . and we
see his hand – lying limp on the cover of* The Magic Camera . . .

*The Policemen hurry into the room . . . They stare motionless at what
they see . . .*

CLOSE SHOT *of Helen – her face buried in her hands.*

*The child's screaming stops suddenly . . . and in the absolute silence
which follows we hear the voice of Mark's father:*

FATHER'S VOICE

Don't be a silly boy . . . there's nothing to be afraid of –

And a small voice answers.

CHILD'S VOICE
Good night, Daddy –

The spotlights begin to dim . . . The dazzling white of the 16mm screen fades slowly into greyness . . .

The room is filled with the gentle breathing of a small child.